"The best primer ever written on t[...] book is cogent and extremely pati[...] erature on the topic into a reader-f[...]"

—Stephen Hinshaw, Ph.D., editor of *Psychological Bulletin* and chair of the department of psychology at the University of California, Berkeley

"This is a very practical guide for patients and their families that provides an excellent framework for understanding bipolar disorder and what can be done to minimize its impact. The book demystifies the illness and explains how to get started on treatment and maximize all of your resources. It will empower patients to find the most comprehensive treatment for their illness."

—Geoffrey A. Wiegand, Ph.D., attending psychologist at Seattle Children's Hospital

BIPOLAR
101

Identifying Triggers, Managing Medications,
Coping with Symptoms, and More

RUTH C. WHITE, PH.D., MPH, MSW
JOHN D. PRESTON, PSY.D., ABPP

New Harbinger Publications, Inc.

Publisher's Note

Care has been taken to confirm the accuracy of the information presented and to describe generally accepted practices. However, the authors, editors, and publisher are not responsible for errors or omissions or for any consequences from application of the information in this book and make no warranty, express or implied, with respect to the contents of the publication.

The authors, editors, and publisher have exerted every effort to ensure that any drug selection and dosage set forth in this text are in accordance with current recommendations and practice at the time of publication. However, in view of ongoing research, changes in government regulations, and the constant flow of information relating to drug therapy and drug reactions, the reader is urged to check the package insert for each drug for any change in indications and dosage and for added warnings and precautions. This is particularly important when the recommended agent is a new or infrequently employed drug.

Some drugs and medical devices presented in this publication may have Food and Drug Administration (FDA) clearance for limited use in restricted research settings. It is the responsibility of the health care provider to ascertain the FDA status of each drug or device planned for use in their clinical practice.

Distributed in Canada by Raincoast Books

Copyright © 2009 by Ruth C. White and John Preston
New Harbinger Publications, Inc.
5674 Shattuck Avenue
Oakland, CA 94609
www.newharbinger.com

Cover design by Amy Shoup; Text design by Michele Waters-Kermes; Acquired by Melissa Kirk; Edited by Nelda Street

---

Library of Congress Cataloging-in-Publication Data

White, Ruth C.
  Bipolar 101 : a practical guide to identifying triggers, managing medications, coping with symptoms, and more / Ruth C. White and John D. Preston.
    p. cm.
  Includes bibliographical references.
  ISBN-13: 978-1-57224-560-0 (pbk. : alk. paper)
  ISBN-10: 1-57224-560-3 (pbk. : alk. paper) 1. Manic-depressive illness--Popular works. 2. Manic-depressive illness--Handbooks, manuals, etc. I. Preston, John D. II. Title.
  RC516.W45 2009
  616.89'5--dc22

                    2008039808

11   10   09

10   9   8   7   6   5   4   3   2   1   First printing

Madness
Lurks around the edges of my mind,
Watching, waiting
For me to let my guard down
So it can invade.
Or perhaps…
Madness will creep in
Under the cover of my denial.
I close my eyes and try to wish it all away.
But I'm no genie.
My genies are pink and yellow and green and white.
And they must escape their bottles often.
Or madness moves in and stays.

—Ruth White
May 19, 2005

Contents

CHAPTER 9

CHAPTER 10

Acknowledgments

I offer thanks to my incredibly talented medical team at Group Health Cooperative in Seattle, including my psychiatrist Dr. Donna Lohmann, my psychotherapist Mike Welsch, MSW, and retired psychiatric nurse Mary Louise. From them I learned how to survive and thrive while living with bipolar disorder, and the ten steps in this book grew out of the years of care they have given and continue to give me. Skilled, patient, kind, and supportive, they taught me to trust my instincts and believe in myself.

To the members of the online support group at DailyStrength .org, thank you for your stories, support, and ideas. Thanks to National Alliance on Mental Illness (NAMI) and Depression and Bipolar Support Alliance (DBSA) for providing me with support and up-to-date information, and also for giving me the opportunity to influence policy affecting services to the mentally ill.

Thanks to my students for being patient, caring, and understanding and for giving me the freedom to be me by accepting me as I am.

Thanks to Dr. Steve Hinshaw, dean of the Department of Psychology at the University of California, Berkeley, who believed, and helped me believe, that my story could benefit the profession and those living with bipolar disorder.

Thanks to Kristen, Geoff, Donna, Sanyu, and Melissa for taking care of Maya and me when I could barely take care of myself. Thanks to Keith for your love, kindness, gentleness, support, and acceptance. Lastly, I thank my daughter Maya, who believes that no matter how crazy our world gets, I am still the best mommy in the world; and if I am, it is because she is my reason for living when all other reasons seem to no longer apply.

—Ruth C. White

Introduction

Before we get started, let's acknowledge that there's no *easy* way to manage bipolar disorder, but there are simple steps you can take to alleviate and manage symptoms. You don't have to do all ten steps in this book to feel better, but the more of them you do, the better your chances of feeling better and getting healthy. Any one of them has the potential to improve your life with this often disabling disorder.

Finding out that you have an incurable, chronic, and serious mental illness is a difficult thing to deal with. Dr. White knows; she's been there. It took Dr. White years to accept that she had bipolar disorder. Being mentally ill brings so much shame because of the social stigma and the preconceived notions people have of what mental illness looks like. Anger is a normal reaction to learning that you'll have to deal with an illness for the rest of your life and that, although you can control some of your symptoms, often things will happen outside of your control that you'll just have to learn to deal with. Dr. White had to learn that being ill was nothing to be ashamed of. She had to learn to let go of the anger, because it was not a very productive use of her energy and often got in the way of her healing. Yet sometimes Dr. White still gets angry, hopeless, frustrated, confused, and out of control. But she has also been hopeful, energetic, happy, and even-keeled.

You may have also experienced the damaged relationships, job loss, poor school performance, substance use, and other negative outcomes that can result from having bipolar disorder. Perhaps you've had your symptoms a long time, or maybe you've just begun to suspect that you have this illness.

BIPOLAR DISORDER CAN BE MANAGED

We hope that, as you read this book, you find that bipolar disorder is not the worst thing in the world to happen to you. It can be treated, and you can lead a productive life. You share a diagnosis with many famous, brilliant, and, yes, mentally ill people. Some have become famous, in part, because of their illness. Others have been brilliant despite or, some may say, because of it. Not all people with bipolar disorder hurt themselves or require hospitalization. Some find relief of their symptoms through treatment and symptom management. Others, have had episodes that required hospitalization, but they were able to return to a productive life when an appropriate treatment plan was followed. Although some people with bipolar disorder attempt suicide, it does not have to be that way. This is why it's so important to manage your symptoms and find good treatment.

Taking Control of Your Life

It's also important to remember that you can go years without symptoms and that bipolar disorder is not one lifelong roller-coaster ride. Although some people feel overwhelmed and have difficulty finding effective treatment or have a hard time managing symptoms, others are motivated, despite their struggles, by a desire to be symptom free, so they work hard to find the treatments that are right for them. Sometimes this may mean participating in trials for new treatment, and other times it means recruiting friends and family to provide the support you need to successfully manage your most difficult symptoms.

For those of us with bipolar disorder, whether we're in a period of wellness or illness, there's so much we can do to divert disaster. And if you're a friend or family member of someone who has bipolar disorder, you'll find that there's also a lot you can do to help your loved one get well and stay well. Bipolar disorder can be a frightening diagnosis when you learn the statistics. According to Kay Jamison of the Johns Hopkins University School of Medicine (2000), at least 25 to 50 percent of people with bipolar disorder attempt suicide at least once, and mood disorders (including depression) are the most common psychiatric conditions associated with suicide. Getting well takes work, commitment, effort, and time. But the payoff of wellness is very much worth it.

How This Book Can Help

Even though Dr. White is a social-work professor with mental illness who has worked with mentally ill adolescents and adults for many years, it took her a long time to finally get a handle on this complicated, serious, and chronic illness. Because of her experience with, and academic knowledge of, this illness, she decided to write a straightforward, comprehensive yet short book about bipolar disorder for people with this condition and the people who care about them.

This is the book she wishes she had when she was first diagnosed. It's the book she still wants to have almost four years later. Because there was nothing in the "short and sweet" category of the market, we decided to write this book and give you what she wishes she'd had: an easy-to-read, straightforward, scientifically based, go-to guide with a friendly tone from someone who knows what it's like to have bipolar disorder.

You may have taken a long road to finally get diagnosed. You may feel relieved that at least you know what's going on with you. You may be in deep denial. You may feel scared about what comes next. You may be angry at the world and at yourself. Maybe you're worried about how to change your lifestyle. Or maybe you're worried about if, and how, you can and should tell your loved ones.

All of these feelings are healthy reactions to a difficult situation. But don't get stuck in these negative emotions when you get caught up in a whirl of medications, blood tests, support groups, and therapy sessions. This book will help you deal with all of those feelings even though it's not a book about feelings. It's an action book. It's a book that gives you steps toward wellness that you can take at your own pace. It may be one step at a time, literally and figuratively. Slowly but surely, with hard work, commitment, and determination, you will find a program that works for you most, if not all, of the time. The goal is to be in remission for the long term (which means doing what works), and to take action quickly and successfully when symptoms break through.

WHAT TO EXPECT FROM THIS BOOK

This book has no complicated scientific discussions and no rigid program to follow. There are some simple writing assignments that will help you learn about your illness and build coping skills. This ten-step guide gives you simple advice based on the latest research to help you manage your life with bipolar disorder. Each step is taken from the latest scientific information and the best practices of mental health, and is written in language that won't overwhelm or confuse you.

Each step helps you maintain your mental well-being and requires you write in a journal or log. Of course, you may not be able to do all ten steps at once. If you're depressed, you may not feel up to doing any of the action steps, even though they can really help you feel better. However, you'll still benefit from the information provided, so reading this book will still help you even if you choose not to keep a journal or log at this time.

You may start at any step and add any of the others as you go. Gaining a victory in one step will motivate you to take on other steps. It's never too late to start any of these steps, and if you stop, you can always start again. Some steps may work for you and others may not. No matter how ill you are, doing any of the ten steps will improve your symptoms and your life.

HOW TO USE THIS BOOK

The book begins with an overview of bipolar disorder, because you have to learn all you can about your illness before you can take on managing your life with it. Becoming educated is the first step to getting better. For more information, you can read any of the articles or books listed in the references section at the end of this book.

Keeping a Journal and Log

To take advantage of the exercises and information in this book, you should have a journal and pen so you can write answers to questions, keep track of symptoms, write your feelings, and make plans for the future. This journal will help you track your progress toward wellness and give you feedback so that you can adjust your use of the steps as necessary. You will also need a three-ring binder and a hundred-sheet package of three-hole, lined paper to log your moods, triggers of bipolar episodes, and diet and exercise habits. The binder will have three sections: one for "Moods and Triggers," one for "Food," and one for "Exercise."

Goal Setting

Goal setting is part of getting healthy, and this book will help you set goals and develop strategies for meeting them. Of course, the overall goal is to get and stay healthy, and the ten steps outlined in this book will help you get there. Writing down goals helps you reach them by making them concrete and reminding you of where you want to go and what you want to do.

ACTION STEP:
Make a Contract Affirming Your Commitment

As a commitment to your own mental health, it may be a good idea to sign a contract with yourself that puts in writing your willingness to work toward getting healthier. You can then take this contract and post it on your bathroom mirror, or keep it in your wallet or purse or on your bedside table to remind you of the work you plan to do to stay healthy. Write this contract in the front of your journal to remind you of why you are keeping it.

Contract with Myself

I, _____ *(your name)*, will read this book and learn how bipolar disorder affects me and those closest to me. I will learn and incorporate into my life at least one step outlined in this book. If I begin to experience bipolar symptoms, I will speak with my mental health provider and seek out my support system for assistance. If I feel I may be a danger to myself or others, I promise to call a crisis hotline, 911, or my mental health provider.

Signed _____ *(signature)* in _____ *(city)* on _____ *(date)*.

Friend or Family Contract

If you are a family member or friend, you may decide to sign the following contract:

I, _____ *(your name)*, do promise to support _____ *(name of loved one)* by encouraging him or her to seek treatment and follow the treatment plan. I will learn to identify symptoms and triggers, set realistic expectations for _____ *(name of loved one)*, and seek social support for myself through support groups or other strategies. I will support my loved one in developing and maintaining coping strategies that will help manage his or her symptoms.

Signed _____ *(signature)* in _____ *(city)* on _____ *(date)*.

CHAPTER 1

Understand Bipolar Disorder

This chapter will give you a broad research-based overview of bipolar disorder, including its symptoms, course, diagnosis, treatment, and management, as well as state-of-the-art knowledge gleaned from reliable sources such as the National Institute of Mental Health, classic texts, and current academic literature.

WHAT IS BIPOLAR DISORDER?

You may ask, what's the difference between the blues, happiness, or depression and bipolar disorder? Although everyone has shifts in mood (for example, anger, sadness, or happiness) related to his or her surroundings and life circumstances, people with bipolar disorder (also known as *manic-depressive illness*) experience unusual, and sometimes drastic, shifts in mood, energy, thoughts, behavior, and ability to function that are out of proportion or unrelated to their environments. Moods swing from extremely high or irritable to sad and hopeless with short or extended periods of stable mood in between. These shifts in mood are called *episodes* and are chronic (that is, recurrent over time) and severe in intensity of symptoms.

THE CAUSES OF BIPOLAR DISORDER

The use of new brain-imaging technology, such as magnetic resonance imaging (MRI), positron-emission tomography (PET), and functional magnetic resonance imaging (fMRI), have begun to give clues to the process of bipolar disorder in the brain. These technologies have revealed differences in the brains of people with bipolar disorder and those of people without the disease.

The body of research on bipolar disorder points to instability in the transmission of nerve impulses in the brain, which is related to the brain's biochemistry. This tendency toward mood instability is considered to be genetically transmitted. People with this biochemistry are more vulnerable to emotional and physical stresses, and the negative impact of stress on treatment is reduced effectiveness. Stress is also a major trigger for the onset of symptoms (Kleindienst, Engel, and Greil 2005).

Although the cause of the disease has not yet been identified, the known triggers for episodes are amenable to intervention and prevention. The major triggers are lack of sleep and high levels of stress. Trauma has also been known to trigger bipolar episodes.

Trauma and Bipolar Disorder

Recent studies have found that childhood trauma does not directly cause—but does hasten—the onset and severity of bipolar disorder. Children who had been abused were more likely to have early onset, in adolescence or earlier (Leverich and Post 2006; Garno et al. 2005).

ACTION STEP 1.1: Assessing Your Experience of Past Trauma

Consider writing about any past history of childhood trauma in your life. However, if this trauma still negatively affects your life, you should only consider doing this exercise under the supervision of a mental health practitioner, because it may be emotionally difficult. If you feel ready to write about your experiences, do so in as much detail as possible, mentioning times, places, people, and details of what occurred. Dealing with this trauma can often be a significant piece of treating your bipolar disorder and may help explain other symptoms or co-occurring mental illnesses that you may have. You will want to discuss this with your mental health care provider or in a self-help group.

UNDERSTANDING YOUR BIPOLAR DISORDER

Increasing your knowledge about your illness and doing the series of exercises in this book will help you better understand bipolar disorder and its impact on your life. Doing these exercises gives you useful information that you can share with your mental health care provider, and it also can help you manage your symptoms, avoid your triggers, and get control of your life. First, start to understand your emotions, because bipolar disorder is about swings between extremes of the emotional spectrum. Keeping track of your emotions will help you see patterns that can be useful in deciding how and where you can make changes in your life that might relieve you of some of bipolar disorder's devastating impacts.

Normal Mood Changes or Bipolar Disorder?

The most marked symptom of bipolar disorder is *significant* shifts in mood from a high feeling, sometimes associated with irritability (mania), to sometimes-severe feelings of sadness and hopelessness (depression).

These episodes can occur over years or within weeks, days, or even hours, depending on the rate of cycling, the period between mood swings. Symptoms for episodes can be mild, moderate, or severe. The various mood states can be viewed as on a continuum, with people who have bipolar disorder experiencing the extremes of the range.

SYMPTOMS OF MANIA

According to the *Diagnostic and Statistical Manual of Mental Disorders*, fourth edition (*DSM-IV*), the official diagnostic manual of the American Psychiatric Association (APA), a manic episode is diagnosed if an elevated mood is accompanied by three or more of the below-listed symptoms most of the day, nearly every day, for one week or longer. If the mood is irritable, then four additional symptoms listed below are required before a diagnosis can be made (APA 2000).

A mild or moderate level of mania is called *hypomania*. In this state, the person feels good, may be more productive and function better than usual, and will tend to deny that anything is wrong, even when others around him or her learn to recognize the symptoms and confront the person with them. Episodes of hypomania often only last two to three days but can continue for a longer period. However, if left untreated, hypomania can develop into severe mania or switch to depression. Someone in a hypomanic state may stop taking his or her medications because of the good feelings associated with this type of episode.

The signs and symptoms of mania are as follows (Frances, Docherty, and Kahn 1996; NIMH 2001):

- Increased energy, activity, and restlessness

- Excessively high, overly good, euphoric mood

- Extreme irritability

- Racing thoughts and very fast talking that jumps from one idea to another so that others having difficulty following your thinking

- Distractibility, inability to concentrate well, or shifts of attention among many topics in just a few minutes

- Needing little sleep yet possessing much energy

- Having an inflated feeling of power, greatness, or importance or an unrealistic sense of your abilities

- Poor judgment

- Going on spending sprees

- Engaging in unusual behavior over a long period

- Increased sexual drive and risky sexual behavior

- Abuse of drugs, particularly cocaine, alcohol, and sleeping medications

- Provocative, intrusive, or aggressive behavior

- Denial that anything is wrong

ACTION STEP 1.2: Assessing Your Lifetime Experience of Mania

In your journal, answer the following questions about your life up to this point:

1. Which symptoms of mania have you ever had and when did they occur? (Write down the month and year of each occurrence; if you cannot remember exactly, estimate.)

2. Approximately how long did these symptoms last (days, weeks, months)?

3. How severe were your symptoms for each occurrence? (Use a scale of 0 to 10, with 10 being the most severe.)

4. How did these symptoms express themselves (problems at work, shopping spree, making multiple and risky sexual advances to people, sleeplessness, and so on)?

5. What was the outcome of these behaviors (interpersonal conflict, moving violation for speeding or reckless driving, and so on)?

This information will help you assess your lifetime experience with mania and will help your mental health provider to understand the nature of your illness. You may also begin to see patterns that will help you change your behavior and thus reduce your symptoms.

SYMPTOMS OF DEPRESSION

For a diagnosis of depressive episode, five or more of the symptoms listed below must last most of the day, nearly every day, for a period of two weeks or longer (NIMH 2001):

- Lasting sad, anxious, or empty mood

- Feelings of hopelessness or pessimism

- Feelings of guilt, worthlessness, or helplessness

- Loss of interest or pleasure in activities once enjoyed, including sex

- Decreased energy or a feeling of fatigue or of being slowed down

- Difficulty concentrating, remembering, or making decisions

- Restlessness or irritability

- Too much sleep or inability to sleep

- Change in appetite and/or unintended weight loss or gain

- Chronic pain or other persistent bodily symptoms not caused by physical illness or injury

- Thoughts of death or suicide, or suicide attempts

Although everyone has low feelings at times, clinical depression is chronic and can be severe, moderate, or mild. In its most severe form, it can be dangerous, because it often precedes suicidal thoughts or actions. It is depression that often brings people into treatment because of the difficulty in functioning that pervades one's life. When mild forms of depression are chronic, it is called *dysthymia*. (Though mania can also lead to suicidality, mania is also marked by denial, which makes it less likely for someone to seek treatment.)

One bipolar patient described a depressive episode like this: "I am tortured by my thoughts, stuck on the theme of death— my death. I want to be dead ... I've had three crying spells this evening, triggered by nothing but overwhelming sadness."

ACTION STEP 1.3: Assessing Your Lifetime Experience of Depression

In your journal, answer the following questions about your life up to this point:

1. Which symptoms of depression have you ever had and when did they occur? (Write down the month and year of each occurrence; if you cannot remember exactly, estimate.)

2. Approximately how long did these symptoms last (days, weeks, months)?

3. How severe were your symptoms for each occurrence? (Use a scale of 0 to 10, with 10 being the most severe.)

4. How did these symptoms express themselves (for example, problems at work, sleeplessness, sleeping too much, lack of appetite, suicidal thoughts, and so on)?

5. What was the outcome of these behaviors (for example, interpersonal conflict, missed work, inability to perform household duties, and so on)?

As with the information about mania, this information will help you understand how depression has affected your life so that you can start considering what steps to take to change your behavior in ways that minimize your symptoms. Your mental health care provider will also use this information to help make decisions about diagnosis and treatment.

SYMPTOMS OF A MIXED BIPOLAR STATE

Some people with bipolar disorder experience a condition called a *mixed state*, which may also be called a *mixed episode, dysphoric mania*, or *agitated depression*. A mixed state is a condition where symptoms of both mania and depression occur simultaneously. Feelings of sadness and hopelessness may occur at the same time as increased energy. Agitation, insomnia, appetite changes, suicidal thinking, and psychosis may be symptoms of a mixed state. One example may include feeling agitated during a depressed episode. It can be an extremely frustrating experience, because it's challenging to describe your feelings to anyone and it becomes difficult to manage your symptoms because you feel so out of control.

One person with bipolar disorder described a mixed state this way: "I'd had a lot of anxiety with marked periods of depression. I felt as if my brain were on fast-forward. I couldn't focus, I wasn't sleeping, and I felt out of control emotionally."

ACTION STEP 1.4: Assessing Your Lifetime Experience of Mixed Symptoms

In your journal, answer the following questions about your life up to this point:

1. Which symptoms of mania and depression have you ever had together and when did they occur? (Write down the month and year of each occurrence; if you cannot remember exactly, estimate.)

2. Approximately how long did these symptoms last (days, weeks, months)?

3. How severe were your symptoms for each occurrence? (Use a scale of 0 to 10, with 10 being the most severe.)

4. How did these symptoms express themselves (for example, irritability, anxiety, thoughts of self-harm, and so on)?

5. What was the outcome of these behaviors (for example, interpersonal conflict, self-harm, missed work, and so on)?

THE DIFFERENT TYPES OF BIPOLAR DISORDER

There are several diagnoses that describe bipolar disorder. Bipolar I disorder is considered the classic form of the disease and is marked by recurrent episodes of mania and depression with possible mixed episodes (Frances, Docherty, and Kahn 1996). Bipolar II disorder is marked by milder episodes of hypomania that alternate with major depressive episodes with no full manic episodes (NIMH 2001). Rapid-cycling bipolar disorder is the diagnosis given when a person experiences four or more depressive or manic episodes within a twelve-month period.

Rapid-Cycling Bipolar Disorder

Some people have multiple episodes within a single week or day, which is diagnosed as *ultra-rapid cycling*. While rapid cycling is more likely to develop in women and in the late stages of the illness, it also can occur in men and can be present in early-onset cases. According to recent studies, approximately 10 to 24 percent of patients with bipolar disorder exhibit this form of the disease (Reilly-Harrington et al. 2007). Rapid cycling is often caused by an interaction between bipolar disorder and concurrent substance abuse (Strakowski et al. 2007; Frye and Salloum 2006), use of antidepressants (Schneck 2006), or thyroid disease (Gyulai et al. 2003).

Severe and Mixed Symptoms

Psychosis may accompany severe episodes of either mania or depression. The common symptoms of psychosis are *delusions* (passionate yet highly unrealistic beliefs, not influenced by logical reasoning or explained by cultural concepts such as traditional religious beliefs) and *hallucinations* (seeing, hearing, or sensing things that are not there). Experiencing these symptoms may result in a misdiagnosis of schizophrenia, which is another severe and chronic mental illness.

Sometimes symptoms can occur together; for example, high energy, depression, and suicidal thoughts. As mentioned above, this is called a mixed state, or dysphoric mania.

Whether or not you've been diagnosed with bipolar disorder, if you suspect that this is a possibility, it's a good idea to track your emotions for at least two weeks (thirty days is better), paying special attention to the time and circumstances surrounding your feelings and any changes that occur.

This information will be helpful for you in your attempts to manage your symptoms and change your life, and it will also help your mental health care provider understand what may be triggering your mood changes. For example, if walking into your workplace every day changes your mood, you may want to explore the reason: Is going to work stressful for you? Do you feel overwhelmed?

Once you understand the root of your unhealthy mood change, you can take steps to prevent it. As you continue through this book, you'll find systematic ways to log your moods that allow better monitoring of them. However, you may also want to write in a journal, which can feel cathartic and provides more information than a number or a check in a box.

Your log can be helpful if you haven't yet been diagnosed but plan to seek mental health care. The information you record will help you understand your day-to-day feelings and take steps toward experiencing more positive emotions and fewer negative ones. It will also help your mental health care provider understand the intensity and duration of your emotions.

ACTION STEP 1.5: Bipolar Symptom Tracking Charts—Depression, Mania, and Mixed Symptoms

Make a two-column table to help you keep track of the presence of any bipolar symptoms on a daily basis, and keep this for at least two weeks. Each symptom for depression, mania, and mixed symptoms will be listed in the first column. In the second column, rate the intensity of the symptom for that day on a scale of 0 to 10, with 0 being not applicable and 10 the most intense.

You can reproduce this chart in your binder or copy the one in this book and fill one out for each day (at least two weeks' worth of pages).

Depression Symptoms	Intensity
Lasting sad, anxious, or empty mood	
Feelings of hopelessness or pessimism	
Feelings of guilt, worthlessness, or helplessness	
Loss of interest or pleasure in activities once enjoyed, including sex	
Decreased energy or a feeling of fatigue or of being slowed down	
Difficulty concentrating, remembering, or making decisions	
Restlessness or irritability	
Sleeping too much or inability to sleep	
Change in appetite and/or unintended weight loss or gain	
Chronic pain or other persistent bodily symptoms not caused by physical illness or injury	
Thoughts of death or suicide, or suicide attempts	

Manic Symptoms	Intensity
Increased energy, activity, and restlessness	
Excessively high, overly good, euphoric mood	
Extreme irritability	
Racing thoughts and very fast talking that jumps from one idea to another so that others having difficulty following your thinking	
Distractibility, inability to concentrate well, or shifts of attention among many topics in just a few minutes.	
Needing little sleep yet possessing much energy	
Having an inflated feeling of power, greatness, or importance or an unrealistic sense of your abilities	
Poor judgment	
Going on spending sprees	
Engaging in unusual behavior over a long period	
Increased sexual drive and risky sexual behavior	
Abuse of drugs, particularly cocaine, alcohol, and sleeping medications	
Provocative, intrusive, or aggressive behavior	
Denial that anything is wrong	

Mixed Symptoms	Intensity
Agitation (with or without depression)	
Insomnia	
Suicidal thinking	
Crying jags (crying for no apparent reason)	
Sadness (mixed with elation)	
Psychosis	

DIAGNOSING BIPOLAR DISORDER

Only a psychiatrist or licensed mental health professional, such as a psychologist, can confirm a specific clinical diagnosis of the type of bipolar disorder you may be experiencing. Keeping your journal up to date and bringing it to any mental health appointment will greatly assist in the diagnostic process. Diagnosis of bipolar disorder is a very complex process and requires the skill of a highly trained professional. You should not assume that having symptoms of bipolar disorder is a diagnosis of the disorder. Neither should you attempt to treat yourself with any medications. You can use some of the steps discussed later in this book to ameliorate certain symptoms regardless of the diagnosis. For example, stress reduction is good for everyone, as are exercise and healthy eating. Just because your symptoms may diminish as a result of taking these actions does not mean you should avoid getting a clinical diagnosis by a mental health professional. Taking effective steps to better mental health begins with an accurate clinical diagnosis.

Because the symptoms of bipolar disorder are so varied and there is no blood test or brain scan to diagnose the disease, it can appear to be something else. Some people think that the mood changes experienced by people living with bipolar disorder happen suddenly, without warning, but in reality, these changes can be very gradual and almost unnoticeable unless you or your loved ones learn to see subtle changes and track triggers that often precede mood changes. Sometimes, because of these subtleties, bipolar disorder goes undiagnosed, especially when substance abuse or other co-occurring disorders exist.

Other times, bipolar disorder can be misdiagnosed, especially as unipolar depression, because people often seek help when depressed and, unless they're asked about possible manic symptoms, that aspect of the illness might go untreated. Similarly, someone experiencing a manic episode may seek treatment and be diagnosed with attention-deficit disorder or attention-deficit/hyperactivity disorder. Some people with bipolar disorder attempt to self-medicate by using alcohol or drugs and may seek help for symptoms related to substance addiction. Poor work or school performance may also be signs of an undiagnosed mood disorder.

Because there's still no biological or medical test for the presence of bipolar disorder, diagnosis is best made by a mental health professional who makes a diagnosis using a thorough case history that includes the occurrence and history of symptoms, along with family history (if available). You can find mental health professionals through various websites, as well as through national professional associations such as the American Psychological Association, the National Association of Social Workers, and the American Psychiatric Association (see the next section, "Resources for Finding a Practitioner"). You can also get a referral through your general practitioner, health insurance company, or health maintenance organization. Make sure to bring your journal with you to your appointment to help your mental health provider with your diagnosis.

RESOURCES FOR FINDING A PRACTITIONER

Several online sources are available to help you find a therapist. You may want to start with practitioners covered by your health insurance company and find referrals from members of any online or in-person support group.

- One very reputable source of information is the referral database at www.manicdepressive.org. The referral site is managed by Massachusetts General Hospital. Also, the search engine at www.mentalhelp.net allows you to search for therapists, support groups, and online communities. It provides mailing addresses, telephone numbers, and Web addresses for these resources.

- The website at www.networktherapy.com helps users find a therapist or treatment facility within a certain distance from their homes. It also provides information on paying for therapists and types of therapy and therapists, and describes how to choose the right therapist. There are also telephone numbers of national hotlines for issues such as self-abuse or self-injury, substance abuse, and suicide. The website also features contact information for support groups, a Web directory, and a list of books.

- A good website for information on finding a therapist specific to bipolar disorder and other mental health conditions is at www.psycheducation.org.

- The online resource at www.findcounseling.com allows users to search for therapists by specialty and location, and provides information on their education. This website is limited in scope and may not provide therapists in locales other than major cities in a few states.

- As mentioned earlier, the following national professional associations can also help you find a mental health practitioner: the American Psychological Association at www.apa.org, the National Association of Social Workers at www.socialworkers.org, and the American Psychiatric Association at www.psych.org.

Now that you have the resources to find a practitioner and know the right questions to ask, your task is to find a provider with whom you can start developing a working relationship. From your list of two or three practitioners, make calls and set up appointments to see them, and bring your symptom tracking charts and list of questions from earlier in this chapter. Set your own priorities, but make sure the person is a licensed practitioner with expertise (whether through education, experience, or both) in bipolar disorder, and select the practitioner who will become your primary mental health care provider. Keep your list and remember that if you find out later that you don't like your initial provider, you can look for someone more appropriate for you.

Screening for Bipolar Disorder

You can also take an online screening test before seeking help from a provider to help you know where you stand. However, these tests should not take the place of getting a professional assessment. Several websites have simple tests that screen for symptoms of depression, mania, and anxiety:

- Depression and Bipolar Support Alliance— www.dbsalliance.org

- Bipolar Screening Test—www.healthyplace.com /Communities/Depression/nimh/bipolar_screening _test.asp

- Screening for Bipolar Spectrum Disorders—www .psycom.net/depression.central.bipolar-screening .html

- Mood Disorders Questionnaire (MDQ)—www .psycheducation.org/depression/MDQ.htm (a highly regarded and widely used instrument for testing the presence of bipolar disorder symptoms)

ACTION STEP 1.6: Find a Mental Health Provider

If you haven't yet visited a mental health provider for a diagnosis but suspect you have bipolar disorder, now is the time to begin the research to find a practitioner who meets your needs. Contact your health care provider and ask for recommendations. Join a support group (online or in your town) and ask members for recommendations. Or, search online for experts on bipolar disorder who are located in your area. The goal is to have a list of at least five mental health practitioners who could potentially diagnose and treat you. You'll want to consider several factors when assessing whether a particular medical provider is right for you:

- Is the mental health provider accepting new clients? (This should be your first question, because if the answer is no, there's no point in asking the remaining questions.)

- Is he or she licensed to practice in your state?

- Does the mental health provider specialize or have substantial experience in treating bipolar disorder? What percentage of his or her practice is made up of people living with bipolar disorder?

- Does the mental health provider accept your insurance, and what percentage of the cost of treatment would be covered by your insurance plan? If you have no medical insurance, ask if there's a sliding-scale payment plan.

If not, ask how much it will cost you. What would be your out-of-pocket expenses for treatment?

■ What kind of education does the provider have? Does he or she have MD, Psy.D., Ph.D. (psychology), or social worker credentials? Where was the provider trained?

■ How long has the provider practiced in your area?

■ Is the provider affiliated with any universities or hospitals?

■ What method of treatment does the provider use? (Look for a combination of medication and psycho-therapy, and encouragement for you to use support groups.) Does he or she use cognitive behavioral therapy (CBT) or some other kind of therapy, and what do these methods entail in implementing your treatment plan?

■ What is the provider's treatment philosophy?

Use this information to narrow down the field to two thera-pists with whom to make appointments so that you can interview them and discern which one best suits your personality. This will be an intense and long-term relationship, so you need to take the care up front to select the best practitioner for you. Only you can judge the responses to the questions above, because everyone has different priorities. Most of all, you'll want to work with someone who is licensed to practice in your state and has a specialization or experience in bipolar disorder (or at least skills in this area, since specialists may be hard to find outside of big cities).

WHO HAS BIPOLAR DISORDER?

According to some statistics (Kessler et al. 2005), between 1 and 2.6 percent of the American population above eighteen years old are considered to be afflicted with bipolar disorder, which is approximately 5.7 million people. Onset of the disease usually occurs in late adolescence or early adulthood but can develop later in life. Children can also be afflicted with the disorder, particularly those who have a parent with the illness. Others are diagnosed later in life, because many patients suffer for years before being correctly diagnosed.

Because bipolar disorder tends to run in families, researchers are looking for genetic markers for the disease, but no one gene has yet been found to be the culprit. Twin studies have shown that several genes and other factors combine to trigger onset of the illness. Children who have a parent with the illness have a one in seven chance of developing the disease (Frances, Docherty, and Kahn 1996).

ACTION STEP 1.7: Know Your Family's Mental Health History

Knowing your family's mental health history will help in diagnosis and treatment of your illness. Because bipolar disorder tends to run in families, this may help clarify whether your symptoms might be bipolar disorder or something else. Bring this information with you to your mental health provider to assist in diagnosis and treatment. In your journal, answer the following questions:

1. Have any members of your immediate or extended family been diagnosed with a mental illness? If so, write down their names, the illnesses for which they were diagnosed, and which, if any, medications you know or suspect they may have taken or are currently taking for treatment.

2. Are many of the symptoms of mania or depression present in any members of your immediate family? If so, what symptoms have you noticed, who are the affected family members, and how are they related to you?

3. Are many of the symptoms of mania or depression present in any members of your extended family? If so, what symptoms have you noticed, who has these symptoms, and how are they related to you?

HOW DO YOU KNOW IF YOU HAVE BIPOLAR DISORDER?

Although you can use self-tests to screen for bipolar disorder symptoms, as mentioned earlier only a mental health practitioner can make a specific diagnosis. The journal and log that you're keeping will assist with this diagnosis by helping your mental health care provider make as informed and precise of a decision as possible, given the nature of the illness. The more details you can provide, the better the chance that your practitioner will make an accurate diagnosis, especially if co-occurring disorders are involved.

BIPOLAR TRIGGERS

A *trigger* is an environmental, biological, or situational factor that causes symptoms of bipolar disorder to begin. Some common triggers are lack of sleep, stress, the change of seasons, inconsistent patterns of eating and sleeping, skipping medications, and changes in normal patterns of exercise, among others.

Your ability to link symptoms to environmental triggers will be the key to managing your bipolar disorder.

THE RISKS OF UNTREATED BIPOLAR DISORDER

Just as the cause of bipolar disorder is not fully understood, there is no known cure for the illness, but it can be managed with medication, education, and psychotherapy, which is the classic three-pronged method for treating the disease. Other strategies for managing the disease include stress reduction, exercise, good sleep habits, and a diet high in omega-3 fatty acids. Thanks to the decreasing stigma of mental illness, more accurate diagnoses, and the availability of better treatments, many people with bipolar disorder can maintain stability and lead productive lives.

Better Social acceptance

Bipolar disorder is a chronic illness with no cure—yet. This means that episodes can occur throughout the life span, from childhood to old age. In between episodes, many people are symptom free, while others have residual symptoms, and a small percentage of people have frequently recurring and severe symptoms despite treatment.

Early diagnosis and appropriate treatment can help people avoid the following negative outcomes (Frances, Docherty, and Kahn 1996).

Suicide: The risk of suicide is highest in the initial years of the illness but doesn't necessarily disappear as time goes on. People living with bipolar disorder have high rates of suicide completion. For some people, suicidal thinking is an ongoing issue that doesn't lead to suicide attempts. The frequency or intensity of these feelings shouldn't influence whether or not you seek help, because it's hard to predict where these feelings will lead. Any thoughts or attempts of suicide should be taken seriously and discussed with a mental health professional. If you cannot access a mental health professional, contact a suicide prevention hotline or an on-call health provider.

Alcohol or substance abuse: More than 50 percent of those with bipolar disorder abuse alcohol or drugs during bipolar episodes. This complicates diagnosis and treatment, and therefore should be addressed if you or anyone around you thinks you may have a problem in this area. Because alcohol and drugs influence mood, anyone who has bipolar disorder should avoid using any illicit drugs and minimize or eliminate alcohol use. If you've already been diagnosed and are on medications for bipolar disorder, you'll find that most, if not all, of your medications caution against using alcohol while taking these medications because of the possibility of dangerous interactions and interference with their effectiveness.

Relationship and work problems: Prompt treatment improves your prospects for a stable marriage and productive work. If it's hard to live with bipolar disorder, it's even more difficult for someone else to live with someone who has bipolar disorder. A spouse or partner requires patience and understanding, and his or her own support system for dealing with the unpredictable ups and downs of living with someone with bipolar disorder.

For those of us with bipolar disorder, work often gets disrupted as our lives and emotions get disrupted. You may or may not choose to disclose your bipolar disorder (this issue is explored later), but episodes play out in work contexts in ways that directly affect productivity. Losing a job is often the outcome of a prolonged episode of bipolar disorder, and this can have a negative impact on the ability to seek or maintain medical treatment. Early diagnosis and compliance with treatment gives you the opportunity to have stable relationships and a productive work life. Having the support and love of people you care about and feeling effective at work are mood boosters that reinforce your treatment. Depressive symptoms are often triggered by the stress of job loss or the loss of meaningful relationships.

Treatment difficulties: Evidence shows that the more mood episodes a person has, the harder it is to treat each subsequent episode and the more frequent episodes may become. (This is sometimes referred to as "kindling," because once the fire has started and spread, it's harder to put out.) Being consistent with your treatment plan and taking the steps to keep your symptoms in check will reinforce itself. As the saying goes, success breeds success. Once you start to feel as if you have some control over your life, you'll start to feel better about your life and be less likely to have anxiety or depression.

Incorrect, inappropriate, or partial treatment: A person misdiagnosed as having only depression instead of bipolar disorder may incorrectly receive only antidepressants without antimanic medication. This can trigger manic episodes and make the overall course of the illness worse. Partial treatment is seen in approximately 50 percent of those under treatment, caused mostly by poor or partial compliance with medications due to unpleasant side effects.

Using your journal in diagnosis and treatment will increase the likelihood of getting an accurate diagnosis and an appropriate treatment plan that reduces episodes, ameliorates symptoms, and has few side effects.

SUICIDE AND BIPOLAR DISORDER

Suicidal thoughts and behaviors can accompany other symptoms of bipolar disorder, and are more likely to occur during the first few years or episodes of the illness. Suicide risk can last a lifetime unless bipolar disorder is properly treated. This is the major reason to get the correct diagnosis and start appropriate treatment of symptoms to reduce the likelihood of severe symptoms. Unfortunately, of all mental illnesses, bipolar disorder has the highest rate of suicide.

Signs and Symptoms of Suicidality

The signs and symptoms that accompany suicidal feelings include (NIMH 2001) the following:

- Talking about feeling suicidal or wanting to die

- Feeling hopeless, that nothing will ever change or get better

- Feeling helpless, that nothing you do makes any difference

- Abusing alcohol or drugs

- Putting affairs in order (such as organizing finances or giving away possessions to prepare for your death)

- Writing a suicide note

- Putting yourself in harm's way or in situations where there's a danger of being killed

One person experiencing suicidal thoughts while in a mixed state described the experience as follows: "Two nights ago I put a knife to my wrist as my daughter slept. It was as if my brain were trying to destroy my body. I think of suicide all the time."

ACTION STEP 1.8: Assess Your Risk of Suicide

Review the above list, and in your journal, write about any suicidal symptoms you have experienced in the past or are experiencing currently. Describe the situations in which these feelings occur or have occurred. Describe the events that preceded these feelings. *If you are currently experiencing these symptoms, call your mental health provider, 911, a crisis line, or the on-call consultant for your health care provider and share this information.* If you experienced these symptoms in the past, share your journal entry with your mental health provider.

GENDER AND BIPOLAR DISORDER

Gender has been found to influence the course of the disease. A major exploratory study of gender and bipolar illness found that women had almost twice the rates of bipolar disorder II as men. Women were also much more likely to have bulimia and post-traumatic stress disorder occurring along with bipolar disorder (Baldassano et al. 2005). The authors also found that women and men had equal likelihood of having a history of rapid cycling and depressive episodes. Other effects of the illness have been linked

39

to gender. For example, a national Canadian study found a link between obesity and lifetime history of mood disorder (McIntyre et al. 2006) that applied only to females. Women in the study who were obese were more likely to have mood disorders.

Because hormonal changes may also influence mood, if you're female, you should include your menstrual cycle data (record which days you're menstruating) in your journal to help you understand what influence, if any, hormonal shifts may have on your moods. Next to your daily tracking of moods, number each day, with day 1 being the first day of your period and so on for one month. This will help you and your provider see if there are any links between your hormonal changes and bipolar symptoms by examining any mood patterns that follow hormonal changes.

Hormonal fluctuations may also be an issue if you are pregnant or in the postpartum period, because many women experience the "baby blues" from a change in hormone levels. However, if the feelings of sadness begin to interfere with your normal functioning, you should consult your health care provider and let him or her know how you feel. Such a change in hormones may also trigger a bipolar episode. Pregnancy and childbirth are risk factors for many women, so make sure to tell your provider about your history of bipolar disorder symptoms, even if you haven't yet been diagnosed.

CONDITIONS THAT CAN OCCUR WITH BIPOLAR DISORDER

Many people with bipolar illness also have other mental disorders. The most common are anxiety disorders, substance use, attention-deficit disorders, and post-traumatic stress disorder. Eating disorders, such as bulimia and other binge-eating disorders, can also co-occur with mood disorders. These equally complex mental illnesses make it more challenging to diagnose and treat bipolar disorder. Compounding this difficulty in diagnosis and treatment is the fact that some of these conditions share symptoms with bipolar disorder. Other mental illnesses must be taken into consideration when a treatment plan is developed. To get appropriate treatment, you must report any use of drugs, legal or illegal, to your mental health provider.

ACTION STEP 1.9: Assess Your Experience with Other Mental Health Conditions

In your journal, answer the following questions:

1. What other mental health conditions have you been diagnosed with, if any?

2. How often do you experience these symptoms (daily, weekly, monthly)?

3. What medications are you taking for these conditions?

For example, you may want to record any experiences of anxiety you have and describe the situation in which they occurred. If you have an eating disorder, you may also want to describe your behaviors around food. Keep track of your intake of alcohol or non-prescribed medications.

Because some of these conditions may also be triggers, we will explore these issues further and help you develop a more systematic way of understanding their role in your bipolar disorder in chapter 4, which focuses on triggers.

In this chapter you learned a lot about bipolar disorder and are on your way to becoming an expert on your own experience with the illness. You've learned about the symptoms of depression, mania, and mixed episodes and now have the tools to track your experience of them. Now that you know about the complexity of bipolar disorder and the challenges it presents in diagnosis, you have a better understanding of the process of seeking help and getting better. You now have a lot of information to give your mental health care provider to help him or her make an accurate diagnosis. You can use this information to see patterns in your symptoms— your moods, emotions, and behaviors—and thus prevent or relieve some of them and start the path to a healthier life.

CHAPTER 2

Get Treatment

The first step in getting effective treatment for bipolar disorder is to get a comprehensive and accurate diagnosis. By taking Action Step 1.6 in chapter 1, you've probably already found at least one mental health provider in your area. The best source for a diagnosis is an assessment by a psychiatrist, psychologist, psychotherapist, or family practitioner. It's best to seek diagnosis from a psychiatrist, a medical doctor specializing in mental and psychological health who can also prescribe medications. You also can get a diagnosis from other professionals, such as your family practitioner, psychologist, or other mental health professional (for example, a licensed social worker or other trained psychotherapist). These other professionals can diagnose you and develop a treatment plan but some cannot prescribe medications. (However, some nurse practitioners and other selected professionals can prescribe medications in some states.)

BECOMING AN INFORMED CONSUMER

A thorough diagnosis should include an assessment of your symptoms and family history. The journal entries you've made so far will be invaluable to your medical provider in making an accurate diagnosis and developing any necessary treatment plan. You need to know your treatment options to make an informed decision, and this chapter outlines the three main strategies used in the treatment of bipolar disorder. Becoming an informed consumer is one way to be your own best friend in your journey to mental well-being.

The more information you have, the more detailed questions you can ask of your provider to thoroughly understand your options and make the best treatment decision, one that will not only give you peace of mind but also work with your lifestyle. The websites listed in the "Resources" section at the end of this chapter, and the books and articles cited in the reference section are other sources of information you can use to help you make the difficult decisions that seeking treatment demands. It's very important that you bring to your first or second visit your journal entries, logs, and an informant (such as a spouse, partner, sibling, or close friend) who can give a more objective picture of your illness. Mental health professionals consulted for this book indicated that they find this information extremely helpful, if not essential, for making an accurate diagnosis.

Health Insurance Coverage

You'll also need to know the scope of your insurance coverage so that you can take this into account when finding a health care provider. Read your benefits booklet and contact your health insurance company's customer service department or your human resources department at work to get answers to any questions you have. Learn whether your health insurance plan covers psychotherapy and psychoeducational groups, and find out the amounts of the deductible and co-payments for visits and medications. This will also help you plan financially for your treatment.

If you have no health coverage, research various options to see what you can afford in the short and long term. For example, ask your provider if a sliding scale or monthly payment plan is offered. Call your public health department to ask for free or low-cost treatment, or ask your provider if he or she can refer you to inexpensive or free treatment programs. When considering treatment costs, include the price of medications, per-visit costs, and any other incidentals. Some pharmaceutical companies offer free or low-cost drug programs for which you may qualify. When assessing the cost, remind yourself of the social, family, career, and personal costs of *not* getting treated and compare that to the cost of treatment. You may save money by not going on irresponsible shopping sprees when manic, or earn more money because you'll take fewer sick days in the future.

THE IMPORTANCE OF SEEKING TREATMENT

Getting treatment is something you do for yourself. It's also something you do for your coworkers, those living with you, your loved ones, and those who interact with you every day. Time and time again, people put off seeking treatment, but generally the longer the illness goes untreated, the more difficult it is to treat. This is why it's important to get professional help as soon as possible.

Seek Treatment for Yourself

Getting effective treatment for bipolar disorder is something you do to give yourself the life you deserve. With proper treatment, you get the chance to make plans and see them through. You can enjoy your life without worrying about getting through each day. You may find that in focusing on treating and managing your bipolar disorder, many of the other problems in your life go away. Relationships with family, loved ones, and coworkers will all improve. Reducing episodes will also save you money on treatment so you can focus on developing your career, building skills through training and education, and pursuing other life goals. You may still experience less severe manias, but now it may result in interesting ideas that you can more easily implement than in the past. If people who are successfully treated with bipolar medications don't stop having episodes altogether, they have them less frequently and less severely. Other benefits of developing and implementing healthy lifestyle changes may be weight loss and improvement of health and overall quality of life.

However, treatment can also mean taking medications with side effects that may bother you. You may miss some of the highs of mania and the bursts of creative energy. You may have to reduce your intake of coffee and skip your late-night glass of wine. At the same time, you may get to smile more often and suffer less from depression and damaging manic episodes. The benefits of treatment far outweigh the pain, suffering, and risks of going untreated.

Seek Treatment for the Sake of Your Loved Ones

Your family and loved ones can relax when you're well, because they need not worry about where you are, what you're doing and thinking, and whether or not you're safe. Your spouse or partner will be free to enjoy your good humor rather than feel the need to protect you from yourself. A depressed spouse is no fun, and a manic one can put a family's financial future at risk and make interpersonal family relationships very difficult. Often one partner is left to cope with all the responsibilities of running a home or caring for children or adult parents. Getting treatment allows you to be a fully functioning player on the family team. You'll probably be a far more welcome guest at family gatherings since you'll no longer be the one "ruining it for everybody."

If you have children, they'll appreciate a present, caring, and calm parent who isn't irritable or emotionally unavailable. Children who have parents with untreated bipolar disorder may often act out due to the parent's emotional instability. Children need adults they can trust, and parents with untreated bipolar disorder are often unable to be good parents, despite their love for their children.

Seeking treatment will make you a better, more caring, and more available parent.

Seek Treatment for Career Success

Your employer and other employees will also benefit from your seeking treatment, because not only will you have fewer absences from work, but you may also be more productive, more collegial, and easier to work with due to your newfound stability, predictability, and trustworthiness. You'll help reduce the costs incurred by your employer from absenteeism and high health care costs. By getting treatment for your bipolar disorder, you'll begin to feel more secure in your employment and more confident in your ability to do your job, which will give you a new self-confidence that expands to other areas of your life, providing an enhanced and more even mood, which may result in less frequent mood changes.

MEETING WITH YOUR MENTAL HEALTH CARE PROVIDER

Once you've decided on a practitioner (following through on Action Step 1.6 in chapter 1), make an appointment as soon as possible (preferably before finishing this chapter or, at the latest, this book) and bring with you all the documents you've created to date: logs, journals, family history, and symptom assessment.

Your First Visit

Your first visit will most likely include compiling a thorough history of your mood symptoms and any other mental health issues through your answers to written or verbal questions exploring your past manic or depressive symptoms. The clinician will ask about your lifetime history with symptoms and whether you have any family history of mental illness symptoms. Bringing a loved one with you to the first session has significant advantages, such as providing support and serving as another source of diagnostic information for your practitioner.

Depending on your past and present experience of symptoms, you may receive a tentative diagnosis after your first session, or the clinician may need more information or have to consult with colleagues. You may have to wait until a second or even third visit before receiving your diagnosis. Because bipolar disorder can sometimes be difficult to accurately diagnose, expect to answer many questions and provide a lot of information. It's not unusual to receive a diagnosis of some other illness before being diagnosed with bipolar disorder, which is why it's so important to have as much information as possible about your mental health history, present symptoms, medication and drug usage, and family history. Put this information in your binder and journal after taking the action steps in chapter 1.

You may leave your first visit with a prescription for medications, or you may have to wait for a conclusive diagnosis. Your prescription may be for more than one medication. You may be referred to a psychoeducation or support group and psychotherapy. Studies of specific psychological treatments for bipolar disorder and psychoeducational groups have shown conclusively that such treatments (along with medications) are far superior to medication treatment alone (Miklowitz et al. 2007). If you don't receive referrals for these major components of a comprehensive treatment plan, ask for them.

ACTION STEP 2.1: Get Informed About Your Treatment

Once you've received a diagnosis of bipolar disorder, no matter whether it's the first or third visit, you'll want to ask your doctor certain questions that will provide you with the information you need to understand the nature of your relationship with him or her and what's required for your treatment plan. Your doctor will give you information that helps you weigh the risks and benefits of various treatments and know what to expect from them:

1. Now that I've been diagnosed with bipolar disorder, what's the next step?

2. What can I expect from treatment in the short and long term (for example, one month, six months, a year, and five years)? What's a realistic goal for me, considering the type and severity of my condition?

3. What methods will be used to treat me?

4. What will this treatment cost?

5. Are there any lifestyle changes I should make that will increase the success of my treatment and reduce the frequency and severity of my symptoms?

6. What method of psychotherapy would you recommend? Are there any support groups you would recommend for someone in my situation?

7. If you're prescribing medications, what are the possible side effects, and how can I ameliorate or prevent these? Is there another medication that would offer the same benefits with different side effects? What should I do if I miss a dose or two?

8. Are you available for consultation by phone or e-mail? If not, is there someone else I can call if I have questions in between office visits? Whom should I call in case of an emergency?

TREATMENT OPTIONS

There's some controversy about the tendency of bipolar disorder to worsen over time if untreated (which, as briefly touched on earlier, has been referred to in the medical literature as the "kindling effect"). This controversial concept proposes that the more episodes someone has, the more likely the person is to have another episode and the more frequent the episodes will get. It's controversial because, although some research evidence supports it, other research contradicts it. Regardless of the progression of the disease, in most cases treatment effectively minimizes symptoms, and increases functionality and productivity in people living with bipolar disorder.

The Stages of Treatment

There are two stages of treatment: acute treatment, which is aimed at ending a current manic or depressive episode, and preventive treatment, when medication, psychotherapy, or both are continued on a long-term basis to prevent future episodes. Acute treatment often requires intensive medication and psychotherapy interventions that stop symptoms from getting worse, with a goal of getting to stability as fast as possible. Once stability is reached, then a more consistent treatment plan can be developed and implemented.

Classic treatment for bipolar disorder includes three main strategies: medication, education (especially regarding lifestyle changes), and psychotherapy. Whatever treatment modalities you choose, *follow your treatment plan!* When feeling good, people with bipolar disorder often tend to deny having an illness. They also tend to discontinue treatment even when it's working, because they feel better and believe they don't need medication. If things are better, stick with the program, because that's a clear sign that it's working. It's easy to tell yourself, "The episode is over now, so I can stop taking my medications." This is a decision that should only be made in conjunction with your health care provider. Although it may be possible to taper treatments over time, in most cases, people with bipolar disorder need ongoing forms of treatment, because the disorder (if untreated) usually gets more serious over one's lifetime.

The Three Strategies of Treatment

Although there are many forms of treatment, this book will discuss the ones provided by conventional medicine (versus alternative or holistic methods): medication regimens, education, and psychotherapy.

MEDICATION REGIMENS

Bipolar disorder is a complex disease that requires medications that often are accompanied by close monitoring of blood levels. A successful medication regimen typically involves trial and error, and demands a close relationship with your medical doctor.

For acute mania the following medications are commonly prescribed: lithium, Depakote (divalproex), Tegretol and Equatro (carbamazepine), Trileptal (oxcarbazepine), and antipsychotic medications such as Zyprexa (olanzapine) or Seroquel (quetiapine). For depression the following drugs are the most frequently prescribed: lithium, Lamictal (lamotrigine), Seroquel (quetiapine), or Symbyax (a combination of olanzapine and fluoxetine). On occasion antidepressants such as Prozac (fluoxetine) may be added on. At times antidepressants can aggravate bipolar disorder and therefore should never be prescribed alone; sometimes they can be used in combination with antimanic agents such as lithium or divalproex. To maintain stable moods and prevent relapse, lithium or Lithobid (a slow-acting version of lithium), lamotrigne, and divalproex are the drugs most commonly prescribed.

Medications for bipolar are often prescribed in combination with each other. A recent large-scale study found that the average number of medications taken concurrently by bipolar patients is three to four (Miklowitz et al. 2007). A combination of medications is most often required for effectiveness and medication tolerability. Antidepressants and benzodiazepines (tranquilizers) are considered risky in treating bipolar disorder, especially if used alone. Lithium usage may precipitate thyroid damage in up to a third of patients taking it for a number of years, so many people, especially women, also take thyroid hormone supplements while on lithium (Fagiolini et al. 2006).

Long-term stability depends on maintaining medication treatment continuously. Those who don't do well are almost invariably people who stop taking medications or take them intermittently or at lower doses than prescribed.

The reality is that many of these medications have significant side effects. Please be very open with your treating doctor about any questions you have regarding side effects. Don't just stop taking medications; this often results in disasters due to the high chance of developing a new manic, depressed, or mixed episode. Often medications can be changed or the dose adjusted to minimize side effects. You are a partner in your treatment with your prescribing doctor. You have a right to bring up any concerns that may arise.

EDUCATION

Getting educated about your illness is an incredibly important step in helping yourself. To get the most effective treatment, you must learn about the disease, its symptoms and treatments, and how you experience the disease. The focus of the first chapter was to get educated about bipolar disorder. However, there are many other avenues for learning about your illness. Because the illness has a unique presentation in each individual patient, one of the ways to learn about it is to keep track of your symptoms (to be discussed in more detail later) and have open and frequent communication with a mental health care provider.

Three excellent online sources for information are the National Institute of Mental Health (NIMH) (www.nimh.nih .gov), the National Alliance on Mental Illness (www.nami.org), and the Depression and Bipolar Support Alliance (DBSA) (www.dbs alliance.org). Many online support groups can help you get information; information on these is provided in chapter 9.

Psychoeducation

Beyond your own reading and discussions with your mental health provider, some treatment modalities incorporate education into their processes. In a psychoeducation model, education strategies are usually integrated into psychotherapy. Psychoeducation is a short-term psychological treatment that most often involves the whole family (and may also include other loved ones, such as a romantic partner). The focus is on learning about bipolar disorder and finding ways for the family to help support the person with bipolar disorder.

Psychoeducation has been found to increase adherence to treatment and improve outcome in bipolar disorder (Gonzalez-Pinto et al. 2004). In fact, those who received six or seven sessions of psychoeducation reduced severe relapses by more than 50 percent. For example, in one study those who received psychoeducation sessions (along with medication treatments) showed a 12 percent rehospitalization rate during a two-year period, compared with a 60 percent rehospitalization rate among those who only took medications (Miklowitz and Goldstein 1990; Rea et al. 2003).

The goal of psychoeducation is to educate people living with bipolar illness to become better at symptom management and increase awareness of the process of their own illness. There are also groups for loved ones who want to learn how to support family members or friends who have bipolar disorder. When conducted in groups, psychoeducation provides support through the sharing of experiences with people who are going through similar struggles. Most psychoeducation programs include information on treatment adherence, early identification of symptoms, and the development of daily routines (Colom and Lam 2005). Research is still under way on the impact of psychoeducation on bipolar disorder symptoms, and at the time of writing this book, the National Institutes of Health was recruiting participants for a study on the impact of structured psychoeducational groups on bipolar disorder.

Support from family and friends is a crucial factor in recovery, and family psychoeducation groups are run by the National Alliance on Mental Illness (NAMI) and the Depression and Bipolar Disorder Alliance (DBSA), where families can learn about the disorder and find help to better support their loved ones' wellness. (See "Resources" section later in this chapter for contact information).

ACTION STEP 2.2: What Do You Still Want to Know About Bipolar Disorder?

In your binder, select a sheet of paper on which to write down *all* the questions you have about bipolar disorder and your personal experience with this illness. Reserve at least two pages for this list so you can revisit it as time goes by. As you learn more about bipolar disorder, you may cross out some questions and add others. You'll want to bring these questions to your therapy sessions, psychoeducation group, or prescribing practitioner. You may even choose to ask these questions in online support forums for people living with bipolar disorder, which we'll explore further in chapter 9, where finding support systems is discussed.

PSYCHOTHERAPY

Psychotherapy enhances the impact of medication in people living with bipolar disorder (Miklowitz and Otto 2006) and reduces relapse (Scott and Gutierrez 2004; Scott 2003) and hospitalization (Scott 2003). It's now unquestionably a viable form of appropriate treatment for bipolar illness (Colom and Lam 2005).

The National Institute of Mental Health (NIMH 2001) states that a combination of medication and psychosocial treatment (which explores how your social environment influences your thoughts and behaviors) is the optimal treatment for managing bipolar disorder in the long term. A review of treatment outcome studies concluded that, in conjunction with medication, psychotherapy reduces the overall rates of relapse but is more effective for reducing episodes of depression than episodes of mania (Scott 2006). In one study, the use of cognitive behavioral therapy had a moderate to large positive impact on sleep, which the authors suggest likely improves other medical and psychiatric measures because of the impact of sleep on well-being (Smith, Huang, and Manber 2005).

Types of Psychotherapy

One review of the research found scientific support for four different psychosocial interventions: cognitive behavioral therapy

(CBT), interpersonal and social rhythm therapy (IPSRT), family-focused psychoeducational treatment, and group psychoeducation (Miklowitz and Otto 2006), with no particular model appearing more effective than any others (Scott 2006; Scott and Gutierrez 2004; Jones 2004).

CBT focuses on specific strategies and exercises that help patients engage in more accurate thinking. It takes particular aim at pessimistic predictions, all-or-none conclusions (such as "I'm totally worthless"), and the common tendency to jump to conclusions (such as "I just know I won't get that job"). CBT techniques are shown to be highly effective in improving critical thinking and combating overly negative thinking (Peden et al. 2005).

IPSRT focuses on a number of the topics covered in psychoeducational groups. In addition, it places particular emphasis on developing lifestyles that are stable and highly regularized (such as eating meals at the same time each day, having specific times to go to sleep and awaken, and so on). In addition, IPSRT emphasizes the importance of addressing potentially troubling and destabilizing relationship problems. This can involve engaging in couples counseling and developing better communication skills.

A review of scientific studies of psychological treatment for bipolar disorders found that certain models have led to increased interest in psychotherapeutic interventions with people living with bipolar disorder (Gutierrez and Scott 2004). It also found that long-term treatment is better than on-and-off treatment for long-term prevention of episodes. The evidence from this review showed that psychological treatment has been linked to a reduction in symptoms, relapses, and hospitalizations and an enhancement of social adjustment and functioning. However, because of the wide variety of variables studied, some therapies were found to be more effective with mania than depression, while others had the opposite effect. They suggest that further studies be done to find standardized interventions that would apply to everyday practice.

Although psychotherapy may have a stigma in some social circles, many people now find that it's not as uncommon as it used to be for someone to seek mental health treatment for a wide variety of conditions. Therefore, the fear of stigma should not prevent you from getting the help you need. Psychotherapy can help you explore your feelings in a safe place without judgment. And with the guided support of a mental health professional, you may learn strategies for overcoming lifelong anxieties or other disturbing emotions.

Whatever mode of psychotherapy works for you is the one you should maintain. Although standard treatment includes talk therapy, you may not enjoy a lot of talking. In that case, maybe it would be best to go to a psychoeducation group where you don't have to say much but can sit and listen to others' stories and focus on specific tasks. Bipolar disorder is not a simple function of biochemistry; it also has to do with the way you think and experience your world. For those of us with bipolar disorder, psychotherapy helps us restructure our thinking so we can perceive and experience our life in a way that won't trigger symptoms. Psychotherapy can also help us maintain stability by supporting the kinds of thoughts that help us stay healthy, improve the quality of our important relationships, and give us strategies for dealing with potentially overwhelming or stressful moments.

You can get treatment for your bipolar disorder and find relief from your symptoms. This requires an accurate diagnosis. The more information you have when you seek a diagnosis, the more likely you are to get an accurate diagnosis. Finding a mental health practitioner with whom you can have a long-lasting, productive relationship takes some research. Once you find some possibilities, ask some screening questions so you can determine the best provider for you. On your first visit, bring as much information as possible. Information to bring along includes logs, journal entries, and your family history. If possible, bring along a friend or family member who can provide an objective assessment of the impact of your symptoms on your life and the lives of others. There are three main types of conventional treatment for bipolar disorder: medications, education, and psychotherapy. For the best outcome, have a treatment plan that combines all three.

RESOURCES

National Institutes of Health—www.nih.gov

U.S. National Library of Medicine (PubMed)—www.ncbi.nlm.nih.gov/sites/entrez?db=PubMed

Depression and Bipolar Support Alliance—www.dbsalliance.org

National Alliance on Mental Illness—www.nami.org

CHAPTER 3

Take Your Medications

It's very important to remember that no matter what medication regimen you're following, you must take all medications *exactly* as prescribed (including dosage; time; and food, water, or alcohol intake instructions) to maximize effectiveness and reduce the likelihood of negative side effects. This chapter gives you strategies that support medication compliance and helps you find your own strategies that work best for you.

GETTING (AND STAYING) MEDICATED

Medication is one of the three pillars of bipolar treatment. Unfortunately, finding the right combination and dosages of medications can involve a lot of trial and error, which can be frustrating. Many people with bipolar disorder must take multiple medications each day to stay balanced, because without proper and consistent medication, they can experience dangerous and unsettling mood swings. This section discusses the importance of adhering to your medication regimen and introduces tools to help you keep it all straight by tracking side effects and working with your doctor to make any necessary adjustments to your medications.

Medication Adherence

The last chapter reinforced the idea that following a treatment plan prescribed by your health care provider is essential to surviving and thriving with bipolar disorder. Aside from the stigma that accompanies mental illness, the challenge of medication adherence often sabotages treatment of bipolar disorder (Colom et al. 2005). A lot of that has to do with the complicated decisions you must make and the blur of various pharmaceutical options that come your way once you've been diagnosed. Even mental health professionals get confused about the myriad options available for treating bipolar disorder. Many manic or depressive episodes are triggered from noncompliance with medication due to either inadvertent or deliberate misuse of prescribed medications. Despite the frustration of finding the right mix of medications, however, pharmaceutical treatment is still the best way to maintain balanced moods in someone with bipolar disorder. Later on in this chapter you'll find tools that can support you in sticking with your medication regimen.

TAKING YOUR MEDICATIONS

There are simple systems for ensuring that you take your medications. These can include some of the following strategies:

- Create text messages to be sent to yourself periodically as a reminder. Some cellular phones and personal digital assistants (PDAs) can be programmed to send text messages at set times. You can also use one of several software programs, such as your e-mail program (Microsoft Office Outlook or Gmail by Google, for example) to remind you, either by e-mail or phone. Some reminder tools are available for free on www.moodtracker.com.

- Set your watch or cellular phone alarm to remind you to take medications.

- Some people put a note on the bathroom mirror to remind them to take their medications, especially if they have to take them at morning and night, which are the two times they are most likely to be in their bathrooms.

- Put a note on your front door that says, "Did you take your meds today?"

- Note the times for your medication dosage as an appointment in your daily calendar or PDA.

- Purchase a pill dispenser that helps remind you of the medication you need to take each day. A pill dispenser also facilitates taking your medication with you in your purse or briefcase so that if you don't go home on a given night or some emergency separates you from your medications, you'll always have a supply of medication with you.

- For people who travel frequently, when crossing borders, it's best to keep your medications in their prescription bottles so that, if you're traveling with controlled substances such as Klonopin (clonazepam), you won't risk being arrested for importation of a controlled substance, because the prescribing information will be on the containers. You'll also want to make sure you put your medications in your carry-on luggage so that in case your bags get lost, your medications won't be lost with them.

- A medication log, described in the next action step, can help motivate you to take your medications regularly while keeping track of side effects and your intake of other substances that may interact with your medications.

SUPPLEMENTS AND COMPLEMENTARY THERAPIES

Many people living with bipolar disorder seek complementary and alternative therapies to help with symptoms. If you're pursuing complementary or alternative treatment for your bipolar disorder, it's best to discuss *all* of your medications, supplements, herbs, and so forth with *all* of your health care providers. This will help you avoid interactions among medications that may impact their efficacy, making drug or supplement effects either stronger or weaker, or potentially causing negative side effects. Please be aware: Just because a product is "natural" doesn't mean it's necessarily safe. A number of over-the-counter and herbal products can have significant and sometimes dangerous interactions with certain prescription drugs. St. John's wort and SAM-e (over-the-counter supplements touted for their antidepressant qualities) have been shown to cause mania when taken by people suffering from bipolar disorder (Nierenberg et al. 1999).

ACTION STEP 3.1: Create a Medication Log

Using a page in your binder, reproduce the table below, or you can photocopy the blank form. Track your medications for a minimum of one month before visiting a prescribing provider to discuss your medication regimen. Include all of the medications you're taking so that your prescribing provider can make the right medication choices for you. Remember that tobacco, alcohol, and recreational drugs can impact the effectiveness of a medication and may carry their own side effects. Therefore it's best if you're as honest as possible about your use of substances other than your prescribed medications.

Write the name of each prescribed medication you're taking in the first column. The prescribed dosage goes in the second column, and the number of pills goes in the third column. Use this form to keep track of how many pills you actually take each day. Hopefully, knowing that you must write down your compliance will help you stick with your regimen. Also record any side effects you experience, such as dry mouth, and to what degree you experience them on a scale of 0 to 10, where 0 indicates you didn't experience that side effect on a given day, and 10 indicates an intolerable level. Also record your intake of coffee, alcohol, tobacco, and any nonprescribed drugs. You can use an x to show that you used that drug or substance on a given day, or you can be more specific and write in how much of the substance you had; for example, number of drinks, cigarettes, or cups of coffee.

On pages 68 through 69 are an example of how a chart might look, and then a blank chart for you to fill out.

Common Concerns

There are many common concerns that you may have about taking psychiatric medications. First, you may be worried that medications will change who you are. Well, isn't that the point? You won't be anyone but you, and you'll be a healthier you—someone who can live life without the uncontrollable mood swings that come and go or their devastating impact on your life. Because you may not feel like yourself anymore, you may be tempted to adjust your dosage without consulting your medical provider. Many people particularly miss the highs and creativity often associated with hypomania. However, adjusting your own dosage is playing with fire.

For example, if you reduced your medication dosage to experience the highs of bipolar disorder, you would also take the risk of experiencing the painful lows of the illness, and the latter may not be worth the former. Your hypomanic symptoms might also morph into full-blown mania. In general, the consequences of your risky medication behavior could mean a return of symptoms and possible hospitalization. Another common concern is the side effects of medications, which can be bothersome, but there are ways to alleviate many of the most troubling ones. If you find them really problematic, discuss your other options with your doctor. The next section further explores this very common issue.

SAMPLE CHART 3.1: Create a Medication Log

Medication Log for the Week of _____ to _____ (fill in dates)										
Medication or Supplement	**Dose (mg)**	**Pills Daily**	**Mon**	**Tue**	**Wed**	**Thur**	**Fri**	**Sat**	**Sun**
Lithium	*300*	*4*	*4*	*4*	*4*	*4*	*4*	*4*	*4*
Clonazepam	*5*	*2*	*2*	*2*	*2*	*2*	*2*	*2*	*2*
Side Effects (0 to 10)									
Dry mouth			*0*	*4*	*0*	*0*	*3*	*0*	*0*

Other Substances

coffee	16oz	12oz	8oz		12oz		12oz

Triggers

	16oz	12oz	8oz		12oz		12oz
Hours of nightly sleep	7	6	8	5	7	7	8
Alcohol and drug use	0	X	0	X	0	0	0
Stress (0 to 10)	2	3	2	8	1	2	1
Menstruation	0	0	X	X	X	X	X
Major life event (-10 to 10)	0	0	0	0	2	0	0
Other:							
Other:							
Other:							

Other Symptoms (0 to 10)

Anxiety	0	X	0	3	0	0	0

CHART 3.1: Medication Log

Medication Log for the Week of _____ to _____ (fill in dates)									
Medication or Supplement	Dose (mg)	Pills Daily	Mon	Tue	Wed	Thur	Fri	Sat	Sun
Side Effects (0 to 10)									

Other Substances																	
Triggers																	
Hours of nightly sleep																	
Alcohol and drug use																	
Stress (0 to 10)																	
Menstruation																	
Major life event (-10 to 10)																	
Other:																	
Other:																	
Other:																	
Other Symptoms (0 to 10)																	

SIDE EFFECTS OF MEDICATION

Unfortunately, bipolar medications can have some pretty uncomfortable side effects, which is often the reason why people with bipolar disorder either don't take their prescribed dosages or stop taking their medications entirely. The most common side effects that influence compliance are dry mouth, weight gain, sexual problems, stomach problems, frequent urination, and appetite changes. However, most side effects can be helped by simple lifestyle changes or by changing dosages or medications, so it's important that you discuss your side effects with your provider. Now we'll discuss the most common side effects and what you can do to alleviate them. Whatever you do, don't make any adjustments to your medication regimen without consulting your prescribing provider.

Weight Gain

Many psychotropic medications, including lithium and Zyprexa (olanzapine), change one's metabolism or appetite and result in sometimes quite rapid weight gain that reduces the desire to continue with these medications beyond the first three months. There are three main ways of addressing the weight gain issue: first, maintain an exercise regimen (see chapter 7); second, follow a healthy diet that's heavy on fruits and vegetables (see chapter 8); and third, talk with your doctor about changing to a different medication.

Dry Mouth

Dry mouth usually results from low fluid intake combined with the frequent urination that accompanies medications such as lithium. The solution is to drink a lot of fluids. Drinking a minimum of eight ounces of fluids every hour that you're awake is essential for beating this very common symptom, which results from the diuretic properties of many psychotropic medications. You may even find that you need more than eight ounces to keep dry mouth at bay. Find your comfort zone and focus on drinking water. Avoid diuretics such as caffeine, which is commonly found in some sodas, coffee, and green or black teas. Some good options are a fifty-fifty juice-water combination (sparkling water gives you a refreshing spritzer), herbal teas, sparkling mineral water, or lightly flavored waters.

Constipation

Zyprexa (olanzapine) and lithium are known to cause constipation. As with dry mouth, drinking lots of fluids is one of the main ways to prevent constipation. A healthy diet filled with fruits (avoid bananas) and green leafy vegetables also serves as a primary prevention. Regular exercise can also help. Constipation is often a problem in the beginning stages of a medication regimen and should sort itself out with the measures described above. If it continues for more than a week despite your best efforts, speak with your prescribing health care provider for further advice. Common treatments include milk of magnesia, suppositories, and Pepto-Bismol. A glass of milk or a cup of coffee also sometimes does the trick.

Sexual Problems

Many antidepressants, such as Prozac (fluoxetine), often cause sexual difficulties such as reduced libido. Discuss these symptoms with your doctor and explore other medication options; for example, Wellbutrin (bupropion) is less likely to produce these side effects. Also note that since depression can also result in low libido, you may want to explore whether your bipolar symptoms are the source of this problem, rather than the medications.

Nausea

Nausea is often caused by taking medication on a full or empty stomach, so make sure you follow the directions exactly as written. If you experience nausea, you may find that eating water crackers or saltine crackers relieves symptoms. You may also want to take your medications with peppermint or ginger tea, or ginger ale, all of which are known to relieve nausea.

Tremors

Tremors are a very challenging side effect for many people because it's a symptom that others can see. Your hands may shake when you write or hold a cup or glass. It's troubling to see this visual effect of the medication, and it can make you feel older than you are due to the association of tremors with old age. Tremors are often caused by the same medications that cause dry mouth, so the solution to tremors is staying well hydrated. If this doesn't relieve your symptoms, speak with your prescribing doctor about other medications that may address your symptoms without this side effect.

Liver and Kidney Problems

Many psychotropic medications, such as lithium, Depakote (divalproex), and Zyprexa (olanzapine), may cause liver and/or kidney damage. Your prescribing provider should schedule quarterly (at minimum) blood tests to monitor your liver and kidney functions. He or she will discuss these results with you and make any adjustments to your medication regimen as needed. The ability to tolerate lithium is greater during acute mania and decreases when these symptoms subside. Other variations in your response to medication may result from interactions with other medications or lifestyle changes. Therefore, discuss with your prescribing provider any changes in your physical condition, such as pain or an increase in side effects. Be sure to meet with him or her on a regular basis, at least quarterly, whether or not you feel okay.

All medications come with some side effects, and if you find that, despite all your best efforts, you have a new health problem that comes with treating your bipolar disorder, you may want to rethink which symptoms are most problematic in your life, your bipolar disorder or medication side effects. If you consider the rate of suicide attempts and completion of people with bipolar disorder and the life disruptions resulting from an episode of mania or depression, then your medications can be considered lifesaving. Once you put it in this perspective, the importance of compliance becomes evident.

TIMING OF DOSES

Some people with bipolar disorder find that the number of pills they have to take and the importance of taking certain pills at certain times of day can be frustrating. It's easy to forget to take a dose, which may begin to trigger manic or depressive episodes. Daytime drowsiness is a major problem with many mood stabilizers and often interferes with compliance because it gets in the way of daily responsibilities, such as work, chores, child care, and so forth.

If you find that you have trouble remembering to take your prescribed doses at certain times of day or that certain medications have negative effects at certain times of day (for example, you feel drowsy in the morning after taking lithium), speak to your provider about rearranging your medication schedule to better fit your lifestyle. You may be able to take different dosages at different times of day, change your medications to alleviate daytime drowsiness, or change medications altogether.

Please review the section "Taking Your Medications" earlier in this chapter for some tools to help you stick to your medication regimen.

ADJUSTING YOUR MEDICATION REGIMEN

As stated earlier, any changes in medication should be done in consultation with your health care provider. Trying it on your own will likely lead to a bipolar episode and all the life-disrupting outcomes that ensue. The good feelings that often are a part of the experience of mania or hypomania lead some people to stop taking their medications, which triggers or exacerbates an episode and may lead to increased severity of symptoms. The goal of treatment is to stay healthy and get off that emotional and psychological roller-coaster ride.

The key factors that contribute to your medication compliance are patience and hope that the medications will work. If you have hope, you'll be motivated to stick with your medication despite side effects, and you also need patience to be willing to make adjustments until you find the medication that's right for you. Medications take time to work, and you may have to try several different drugs before you find one or more that work for you. To keep on the treatment path, stay hopeful that you'll find the right combination of medications that work for you. Use your time in psychotherapy or your support group to learn maintenance strategies and find support for compliance with your medication regimen.

KNOWING YOUR MEDICATIONS

To take your medications as prescribed and trust that they'll work, you must know the medications you're taking and their possible side effects so you can distinguish medication side effects from other medical problems you may have and from symptoms of the illness itself.

In addition to asking your health care provider, you can do your own research on your medications. One good source of information is the online version of the Physicians' Desktop Reference (PDR) at www.pdrhealth.com (also found in print at your local library). The PDR is based on information provided by the U.S. Food and Drug Administration. Simply typing in the name of your medication will get you other names, side effects, actions, indications, how the medicine is supplied, special warnings, and possible food and drug interactions. It's easier to search by brand name than the generic name of the medication. There's also a picture of the medication. For example, when searching for lithium, the PDR shows Eskalith (one of the trade names for this chemical) and lets us know that it's available in pill and capsule form.

Another resource is the *Consumer's Guide to Psychiatric Drugs* (Preston, O'Neal, and Talaga 2009), which describes medical treatments for bipolar disorder in detail.

ACTION STEP 3.2: Know Your Medications

The goal of this exercise is to educate you (and inform your mental health care provider) about *all* the medications you're taking, whether for bipolar disorder or other conditions. For each drug you're taking, you'll record some detailed information. You can use a table format or simply have a paragraph for each drug. Here's the information you'll record:

1. What's the chemical (generic) name of the medication?

2. What's the brand name (if applicable; that is, if it's not a generic drug) of the medication?

3. How much of the medication are you taking? (For example, the number of pills you take each time you take the medication and the amount of medication in each pill; see your medication log.)

4. How often do you take the medication? (For example, twice a day or every four hours and so on; see your medication log.)

5. What's the health problem for which this medication was prescribed?

6. How long you have been taking this medication?

7. What side effects do you think you may be experiencing as a result of taking this medication? (See your medication log.)

Bring your answers to your prescribing provider so that possible interactions can be avoided and prescribing can be based on as much information as possible. Be honest in reporting your compliance with medications, because if it's prescribed but you aren't taking it, this must be taken into account when new prescriptions are made or when your medical provider tries to understand the nature of your symptoms. If you've taken other drugs previously for the same condition, it would be useful to list the names of the drugs you took prior to the current one and why you stopped taking them. Finally, also answer these questions for any alternative medications or nutritional supplements you're taking. All this information helps develop the medication regimen that works best for you.

Discussing Your Medications with Your Provider

Once you've begun to know and consistently take the prescribed medications, you may want to have some discussions with your medical provider about the effectiveness and side effects. The previous action step will help you conduct a very informed discussion with your health care provider about your specific medication needs and experiences. Some side effects are more problematic for some people than for others; for example, whereas one person may be okay with weight gain, others may find it intolerable.

On a regular basis (annually or every six months), talk to your health care provider about the drugs you're taking. At these intervals, discuss side effects, effectiveness of symptom reduction, or any changes in your behaviors. Also ask about any new scientific information on the effectiveness of the drug or any new side effects or risks that have been discovered. You may want to try new drugs that have come onto the market to see if they work better for you. However, you may want to stick with the medication that works for you rather than risk episodes or new side effects by trying something new.

ACTION STEP 3.3: Medication Q & A

Some questions you may want to ask when discussing medication with your mental health provider are as follows:

1. Why am I taking *this* medication rather than any of the other medications that could be prescribed for this condition?

2. What are some of the side effects I will likely experience, and is there anything I can do to alleviate or prevent some of them from occurring?

3. Are there any possible interactions among the medications that I'm already taking? Is there any way to

alleviate or prevent these interactions? Would substituting another medication alleviate or eliminate these interactions?

4. Are there any nutritional supplements, dietary considerations, or behavioral changes that could reduce my dependence on a particular medication?

5. Are there any foods or activities I should avoid while taking these medications?

6. Please give me complete medical information on all the medications you're prescribing for me (*if this was not already done or you no longer have that information*).

Lifestyle and Behavior Changes

Another reason to discuss your medications with your provider is that you may have begun new behaviors—such as quitting smoking, beginning an exercise plan, or practicing stress reduction techniques—that impact the necessary dosage of your medication. For example, regular exercise may reduce dependence on medications for diabetes, heart conditions, anxiety, depression, or mania (Slentz, Houmard, and Kraus 2007; Barbour, Edenfield, and Blumenthal 2007). Eating foods rich in omega-3s or taking omega-3 supplements may improve mood in some people and therefore reduce the need for mood stabilizers (Lin and Su 2007). (We'll explore exercise and nutrition further later in this book.)

Given this new information, your provider may want to adjust your dosage.

If you find it challenging to talk assertively with your medical provider on your own, you can choose to bring a trusted friend to give you a boost of confidence or act as your advocate in getting the care that's best for you.

This chapter discussed how difficult it is to find the medications and dosages that are right for you. However, being an informed and assertive consumer will help you tremendously, because you'll know the right questions to ask when meeting with your provider. You'll be able to advocate for yourself now that you have the information you need about your medications, compliance, side effects, and medication options. Educating yourself about your medications helps with compliance and prevents potentially dangerous interactions with other medications or lifestyle choices. Keeping track of your medication compliance motivates you to comply. It also helps you when you start tracking your symptoms, because you'll be able to see how well your medications work.

CHAPTER 4

Recognize Your Triggers and Track Your Moods

Knowing your triggers may help you avoid symptoms and therefore reduce your medications. Your treatment plan will begin to reflect the amount of control you start to gain over your life with bipolar disorder. Recognizing triggers and tracking your moods are two of the most useful tools for stabilizing your moods, because understanding moods and triggers helps you stay on track with the other steps. For example, when you don't exercise, you can often see the difference it makes in your mood. If you experience a trigger, you can stave off a related mood change by making sure that you take all the steps necessary to keep your mood stable, such as ensuring that you get enough sleep, taking your medications, and seeking out your friends for support. Should you become aware of a mood change while tracking your moods, consider seeing your mental health provider and asking for adjustments to your medications.

WHY GET TO KNOW YOUR TRIGGERS?

It's important to learn what triggers your symptoms so you can understand how to avoid symptoms and perhaps reduce the amount of medication you have to take. Knowing your triggers can help you become attuned to any warning signals that an episode is on its way. Then you can take preventive steps and find the help you need to mitigate the situation and get you through. Understanding your triggers empowers you to reduce the frequency and intensity of episodes, and also gives you hope that you can have some control over your illness. For those of us with bipolar disorder, an illness that often makes us feel powerless, any control we can gain strengthens our self-esteem and sense of self-efficacy. Knowing your triggers and tracking your moods can also help you take some responsibility for your bipolar disorder, putting you in the driver's seat to set treatment and life goals with some hope of achieving them. Tracking your triggers and moods can give you some objectivity and perspective on the nature of your illness. Tracking your moods helps you know the difference between *you* and your bipolar disorder. In the process, you get to know who you are, what makes your illness worse, and what you can do to help make it better. It's the difference between a surprise hit from behind on the highway, and seeing the obstacle on the road in front of you in time to take steps to avoid it.

You'll learn your triggers by reviewing your journal and by observing some of the patterns in the relationships between your symptoms and your behaviors and circumstances. If you've done the action steps throughout the previous chapters, you have a good record of your experience of symptoms and what has preceded and followed each instance. The Depression and Bipolar Support Alliance suggests that people with bipolar disorder keep a food journal to see what foods may trigger mood changes or whether mood changes trigger changes in eating patterns (DBSA 2005). Chapter 8 explores the role of diet and nutrition in balancing moods and reducing bipolar symptoms.

POSSIBLE TRIGGERS FOR BIPOLAR EPISODES

Even though bipolar disorder is highly genetic, which means that you may have an inherent propensity for the illness, an episode is often preceded by a life event or circumstance that triggers it. Some of these triggers may be related to lifestyle. Here are some examples:

- Changes in sleep, with sleep deprivation triggering mania

- Alcohol use, which can trigger depression

- Use of caffeine or tobacco, which can trigger mania

- Use of illicit substances, which can trigger either mania or depression, depending on the drug, with drugs such as cocaine more likely to trigger mania and tranquilizers more likely to trigger depression

- Eating foods high in sugar or having an unhealthy diet

- Missing doses or misusing prescription medications, supplements, or alternative medicines (whether for bipolar disorder or other illnesses)

- Medications including antidepressants and stimulants; for example, over-the-counter cold medications, appetite suppressants, thyroid medication, or corticosteroids

- Lack of exercise, which can trigger either mania or depression

- An irregular life schedule, such as eating, sleeping, and working at different times each day

Some triggers may be environmental or circumstantial. Here are some examples:

- High levels of stress, which can trigger either mania or depression

- Excessive stimulation, which is more likely to trigger mania

- Menstruation, which impacts each woman differently

- Abnormal levels of thyroid hormones

- Changes in seasons and their accompanying light fluctuations, with mania more likely in the summer and depression more likely in the winter

Onset of the illness is also often triggered by major life events that cause stress, which can trigger either a manic or depressive episode, depending on the person and how stress impacts him or her. Here are some examples of stressful life events:

- The death of someone close to you

- Divorce or loss of a romantic partner

- Difficult personal relationships

- Getting married

- Going away to college

- The birth or illness of a child

- Problems at school or work

- Financial difficulties

- A change in employment, such as starting a new job or losing one

- Moving, especially to a new place without an established support system

GENETICS AND BIPOLAR DISORDER

Genetic factors also play a role in how an individual experiences stressful life events (Paykel 2003). Genetic markers are under active investigation, but until we discover what they are, we're left with monitoring the factors we can see. However, having family members with bipolar disorder increases the likelihood that you'll have it too, which tends to be expressed in sensitivity to certain environmental conditions, such as life traumas or substance use, that may trigger bipolar disorder symptoms.

GETTING TO KNOW YOUR TRIGGERS

As previously stated, getting to know what triggers your bipolar episodes can take you a long way toward understanding your illness and learning to manage your symptoms. The next action step helps you identify your triggers so you can learn what situations to avoid and how to manage these situations to reduce your risk of an episode.

ACTION STEP 4.1: Name Your Triggers

In your binder or journal, list past life events or situations that preceded your bipolar disorder symptoms. These are the types of events or situations you'll need to avoid or handle carefully.

Knowing that you'll have to be in any of these triggering situations may be a reason to speak with your mental health provider so you can plan together how you'll manage the situation, including planning how to react to the situation or adjusting your treatment plan in anticipation of the triggering situation's potential effect on you.

For example, after many years Janet and her therapist realized that changes of seasons always resulted in increased visits, particularly in the fall. Once they realized this, they were able to develop a specific treatment plan for Janet to undertake in the fall that included regular exercise, a change in her medications, and the use of a high-intensity light to treat her symptoms. They worked together to prevent another episode by taking action before fall and its early darkness arrived.

To find out what some of your triggers are, look back through your binder and journal for behaviors or circumstances that occurred hours or days before you experienced any bipolar symptoms (review the lists of symptoms in chapter 1). If you haven't kept a journal, simply think back to when you had your last bipolar episode and recall what situations or conditions preceded it. Take a page in your binder and list the categories of triggers below and reflect on how they applied to your last experience of bipolar symptoms. For each trigger write what symptoms you experienced. If you have a hard time doing this, you may want to ask someone who lives with you or knows you well to help you identify conditions or situations that preceded your last episode or another past episode. This will help you and your provider understand the nature of your illness so you can prepare to manage or prevent symptoms before they start.

1. Weather (for example, rainy, cloudy, or sunny)

2. Stress (for example, work or family)

3. Drug, tobacco, or alcohol use

4. Diet (for example, amount of carbohydrates, fruits, caffeine, vegetables, or overeating or undereating)

5. Social life (for example, friendships, family, or late nights)

Now that you've listed some of your triggers, you can look out for these danger signs and start taking action as soon as you see one of these situations coming your way. When you notice you've experienced a trigger, start logging your moods in the chart described below. Consider contacting your mental health care provider for advice on what to do to prevent an episode. Your provider may adjust your medication or suggest lifestyle changes that will prevent or reduce your symptoms. One good way of managing your symptoms is to use the Weekly Moods and Triggers Chart at the end of this chapter to log your daily mood symptoms, treatments, sleep patterns, and life events so you can understand how your symptoms get triggered, how they manifest, and what works in treating them.

ACTION STEP 4.2: Create
Your Monitoring Chart

The following chart expands on the Medication Log in chapter 3. The following guidelines will help you construct a chart for one week. This chart combines elements of many charts that can be found online. The trackers in the online charts are hard to customize, because they already show all the categories, which makes it hard for you to adapt their tools for your needs. Some such websites are run by pharmaceutical companies; other websites charge for their charts; and others, such as bipolar support organizations, provide them for free. The chart in this book is very comprehensive with detailed instructions. You can create your own chart or photocopy the blank one provided.

When you're in the throes of a bipolar episode, the last thing you may want to do is chart moods and triggers. At these times you may find it easier to just jot your feelings in your journal so you can make your chart later. As a last resort, you may choose to simplify your chart to include only the most important information, such as your mood, sleep patterns, medication compliance, and symptoms.

This chart shouldn't cause you anxiety or be a burden, so customize it to fit your life. No matter how you do it, at the very least, it will give you a better understanding of your illness and therefore will help you work toward minimizing the frequency and intensity of your symptoms, and find ways to deal with symptoms as they arise.

1. **Make your chart.** Use graph paper, word processing software, or a spreadsheet program, such as Microsoft Excel, to create a table for each week, or copy the one in the book at the end of this chapter. Have it cover seven days (Monday through Sunday, for example) so you can copy or print it for use in any week of the year. A computer spreadsheet is particularly useful if you want to use graphs or charts to see patterns so you can better understand the relationships between your moods and triggers. It's a good idea to use a computer spreadsheet program, because you can add and subtract items as necessary, and a depiction of your information helps you see the patterns you may not notice when there's a sea of numbers and/or x's in front of you.

2. **Track your medications.** Continue tracking your medications and side effects as you began doing in chapter 3. Remember to list whatever side effects you experience and put an x on the date you experience that symptom. For greater precision in your recording of side effects, rate the intensity of these effects on a scale of 0 to 10, with 0 meaning no experience of that side effect and 10 meaning an intolerable level. If weight gain is a side effect, track it by weighing yourself daily so that you know how much weight you're gaining and at what rate.

3. **Track the number of hours you sleep.** Write the number of hours you slept the *night before* you woke up on that date (for example, if you got eight hours sleep last night, note that on today's date).

4. **Track your use of alcohol and drugs.** Place an *x* in the box if you used drugs or alcohol on that day. You may want to use more precision and record how many drinks (one ounce of liquor, one beer, or one glass of wine) you had that day. This will be especially useful if you already have substance-use issues.

5. **Track your stress levels.** Rate your level of daily stress on a scale of 0 to 10, with 0 meaning a day of no stress and 10 meaning the most stressful day.

6. **Track your menstrual cycle.** For women, put an *x* in the date box if you're menstruating on that date. Hormonal changes due to menstruation often trigger depressive symptoms, even in women without bipolar disorder. However, many women experience no change in symptoms when menstruating. By tracking your monthly cycle, you can see if any changes in your mood precede or accompany your menstrual period.

7. **Track major life events.** If you experienced a major life event (review the list above), place an *x* in the box. For more precise recording, rate the impact this life event has had on your life by rating it from -10 to 10,

with -10 meaning the most negative and 10 meaning the most positive. If this event has had a significant impact on your life, you may want to write more about it in your journal to provide you with more information about the event and how it made you feel.

8. **Rate your mood.** If your mood is stable or balanced, place a 0 in the mood boxes. Rate your experience of depression or mania using the following scale:

Mania	Depression
1 = more energetic/productive; routine maintained	1 = usual routine; not affected much
2 = some difficulty with goal-oriented activity	2 = functioning with some effort
3 = great difficulty with goal-oriented activity	3 = functioning with great effort
4 = incapacitated or hospitalized	4 = incapacitated or hospitalized

9. **Track your mixed symptoms.** Place an *x* on a date if you experience mixed symptoms, which is when you have symptoms of depression and mania at the same time.

10. **Track number of mood changes.** Record the number of mood changes you had during the day. You may have to estimate this number, because it's often difficult to keep track when you're experiencing them.

11. **Track other symptoms.** List other physical and mental symptoms that you experience and place an x on the date you experience them. For more precision, rate the interference of these symptoms with your life on a scale of 0 to 10, with 0 meaning no interference and 10 meaning the most interference.

The following table is an example of how a chart might look, and below it is an explanation of how to interpret your findings. There is a clean copy for your use at the end of the chapter.

SAMPLE CHART 4.2: Tracking Moods and Triggers

Weekly Moods and Triggers Chart for the Week of 4/7/08 to 4/13/08									
Medication or Supplement	Dose (mg)	Pills Daily	Day 1 Mon	Day 2 Tue	Day 3 Wed	Day 4 Thur	Day 5 Fri	Day 6 Sat	Day 7 Sun
Lithium	300	4	4	4	4	4	4	4	4
Clonazepam	5	2	2	2	2	2	2	2	2
Side Effects (0 to 10)									
Dry mouth			0	X	0	0	X	0	0
Triggers									
Hours of nightly sleep			7	6	8	5	7	7	8
Alcohol and drug use			0	X	0	X	0	0	0
Stress (0 to 10)			2	3	2	8	1	2	1
Menstruation			0	0	X	X	X	X	X
Major life event (-10 to 10)			0	0	0	0	2	0	0

Mood							
Mania (0 to 4)	2	0	0	1	0	0	
Depression (0 to 4)	0	0	1	2	0	0	
Mixed states	0	0	0	X	0	0	
No. of mood changes	0	0	0	3	0	0	

Other Symptoms (0 to 10)							
Anxiety	0	0	0	3	0	X	0

Healthy Behaviors							
Exercise	X	X	X	0	X	X	X

Interpreting Your Results

The table you create can provide you with a wealth of information about your behaviors, triggers, and moods. Let's say the sample chart above is the log of a woman named Roberta. If you notice, on the third day of the week logged, Wednesday, Roberta was having a good day. She had a good night's sleep and her stress levels were low. However, on Thursday, the fourth day of the week, she had little sleep and a high stress level, and was beginning to feel low levels of depression. She also experienced anxiety, which she tried to deal with by drinking some alcohol.

Looking for Patterns

As you start to use this tool, begin looking for patterns on a daily or weekly basis. After you get the hang of it (from two to four weeks), you may want to observe patterns on a monthly basis. Lastly, once you have a year's worth of data, look for seasonal patterns as well, because many people living with bipolar disorder also experience seasonal affective disorder (SAD), which is a reaction to changes in sunlight. Keeping track of your triggers and moods, especially from September through November and from February through April, will help you notice whether changes in seasons and sunlight affect your mood.

What you're looking for are patterns linking certain triggers to your moods. You can simply eyeball the chart, noticing the days when you experienced symptoms to determine which of your triggers may have preceded the symptoms. You can also use the absence of symptoms to reinforce healthy and protective behaviors, such as exercise, getting a good night's sleep, and taking your medications as prescribed. Knowing that what you're doing is working really helps motivate you to keep doing it and increases your positive feelings toward yourself. It reinforces the fact that you indeed have some control over your illness.

You may also use a spreadsheet to chart your symptoms in relation to your triggers. This will help you see patterns over time much more easily than when simply looking at the raw information. If you prefer not to use a spreadsheet, you can use graph paper to make a graph that visually demonstrates your results.

Remember, no matter what you do, you still may experience symptoms of your bipolar disorder. It can be very frustrating to continue experiencing symptoms when you think you're doing all you can to manage them, but remember that it's very likely that your symptoms would be more severe and occur more frequently if you weren't taking care of yourself as this book recommends.

MANAGING YOUR TRIGGERS

Although it may seem somewhat overwhelming to track your moods and triggers daily, once you get the hang of it, you'll be able to fill out each day's chart in no more than five minutes. Your stability and mental well-being are worth five minutes a day. You can also continue to write your thoughts and feelings in your journal in more depth. Eventually, as you learn to manage your symptoms, you may find it less important to do all of these steps all the time. Instead, do them as you start to feel changes occurring that you may want to monitor.

Customizing Your Chart

Your goal is to create a monitoring chart specific to your needs, with items that especially relate to your own situation. You can use the list of triggers you created earlier in this chapter as a starting place and add or remove items as needed. The chart is a tool you can use your entire life to help you manage your symptoms and your life. It provides a one-stop source for important information that will help you, your medical provider, and your loved ones support you in living your best life.

For example, if you notice that the seasonal change into fall tends to trigger mixed episodes and some depression, you might choose to carefully monitor your feelings and thoughts during September by both keeping a journal and a chart like the sample above. If you notice yourself beginning to experience consistently low moods, you can take steps to interrupt a depressive or mixed episode. By creating a customized chart that reflects your own triggers and symptoms, you can come to a better understanding of how your bipolar disorder operates and be more aware of potential issues that could trigger an episode.

In this chapter you learned the importance of understanding what triggers your bipolar episodes. Some triggers are based in your lifestyle, changes in your environment, and/or major life events. Understanding what triggers your bipolar episodes may help you avoid them altogether or get them treated early to deter major impairment. You've been given a comprehensive tool for tracking your symptoms and moods, and you've learned what to do with the information once you've collected it, which is to share it with your medical provider and also look for patterns showing links between your triggers and episodes. Customizing this very simple tool to suit your unique experiences will increase its effectiveness so that it can be a central repository for a lot of very useful information. You and your mental health care providers can use this information to develop a more effective treatment plan for you that addresses your particular set of triggers and symptoms. The rest of the book targets minimizing the effects of various triggers with a healthy lifestyle and a support system. Understanding how those triggers work will give you and your medical provider information that will help keep you healthy and stable.

CHART 4.2: Tracking Moods and Triggers

Weekly Moods and Triggers Chart for the Week of _____ to _____									
Medication or Supplement	Dose (mg)	Pills Daily	Day 1 Mon	Day 2 Tue	Day 3 Wed	Day 4 Thur	Day 5 Fri	Day 6 Sat	Day 7 Sun
Side Effects (0 to 10)									
Triggers									
Hours of nightly sleep									
Alcohol and drug use									
Stress (0 to 10)									
Menstruation									
Major life event (-10 to 10)									

Mood																
Mania (0 to 4)																
Depression (0 to 4)																
Mixed states																
No. of mood changes																
Other Symptoms (0 to 10)																
Healthy Behaviors																

CHAPTER 5

Minimize Stress

Most people can recognize the symptoms of stress: tension, feeling overwhelmed, anxiety, anger, frustration, and weight fluctuations due to increase or decrease in appetite. Most of these are really our emotional and psychological reactions to factors in our environments, such as traffic delays, long hours at work, interpersonal conflicts, financial issues, health problems, and major life transitions. We also have physical reactions to stress: for some, it's neck tension and stomach distress; for others it's headaches, back spasms, sleeping difficulty, reduced libido, and constant fatigue.

WHERE DOES OUR STRESS COME FROM?

Much of our stress is from the go-go lifestyle endemic to life in the United States: too much to do and not enough hours in the day in which to accomplish everything on our to-do lists. We get praise for working long hours and living without sleep, but getting insufficient sleep and overworking are not healthy behaviors. Chronic stress can lead not only to the symptoms above but also to more acute and chronic problems, such as heart disease and hypertension. If you're already dealing with these health issues, it's imperative to learn coping strategies that will reduce symptoms and keep you healthy.

STRESS AND BIPOLAR DISORDER

Stress has such an impact on our minds, bodies, and spirits that it exacerbates mental illnesses such as bipolar disorder. Stress is a significant trigger for episodes of bipolar disorder. Obviously, people who don't have bipolar disorder get irritable, impatient, and short-tempered when faced with chronic stress, but for people with bipolar disorder, uncontrolled stress can lead to dangerous manic or depressive symptoms. The degree of stress we have in response to environmental stressors is partly genetic but can be controlled when we learn behaviors that minimize its impact on our psyches, relationships, and bodies.

Both human and animal studies have found links between emotional sensitivity and response to stress, and the predisposition toward mood disorders (Bale 2006). A Swedish twin study found that the relationship between stressful life events and mood disorders was due to a combination of environment and genes. Researchers found that some people with mood disorders tended to be drawn to high-risk environments (Brostedt and Pedersen 2003).

High levels of stress and limited access to social support, such as family and friends, are linked with recurrence of bipolar episodes, particularly in cases of people diagnosed with bipolar I disorder (Cohen et al. 2004). The stress related to a death in the family and other major life events was found to be associated with increased risk of first admission with bipolar disorder (Kessing, Agerbo, and Mortensen 2004). This means that major stress relates to the onset of a bipolar episode severe enough to potentially result in a hospitalization.

Coping with stress has to do with our response to our environments. Having bipolar disorder can be very stressful and creates anxiety that reinforces symptoms. But with psychotherapy and medications that reduce anxiety, those of us who have bipolar disorder can learn how to live in the present moment without worrying as much what might happen *if* we have an episode. When in the midst of an episode, we may feel anxious that it might result in a hospitalization. Though we may feel we have no control over whether or not that happens, learning to cope with our stress in a healthier way helps us focus more effectively on managing our symptoms, which reduces the likelihood of being hospitalized or having a severe episode.

THE STRESS RESPONSE

Our reactions to stress are both common and unique, in that many people share responses to stress, such as increased heart rate, sweaty palms, headaches, and other common symptoms, but we each have our own unique combination of responses. Our stress response is not always a bad thing. For example, the rush of adrenaline you feel during a job interview may keep you sharp and focused, and help you present your best self. Other people may react to that same type of stressful situation with sweaty palms and an inability to focus or concentrate, causing them to fail the interview. We all have stress reactions, but the key is to learn healthy ways to cope with stress rather than engage in unhealthy behaviors that may trigger manic or depressive episodes

Coping with Stress

So how do you relieve stress? Coping with stress requires that you identify and understand the source of your stress and then make a plan for how to reduce the impact of that stressor on your life. The next set of action steps will give you some tools to help you identify stressors, become more aware of your reactions to these stressors, and learn how to cope with triggers so you can reduce the impact of stress in your life. Let's start on a positive note by identifying how you can reduce your stress.

ACTION STEP 5.1: Name Your Stress Reducers

1. Think of five activities you've done from time to time that have brought you peaceful feelings. These may include time spent at the beach, relaxing with your family, reading a book in your favorite coffee shop, taking a nap, or engaging in a hobby, such as knitting or swimming laps in a pool. Open your journal to a blank page and draw a line down the center, dividing it in half.

2. On the left-hand side of the page, list the top five situations that make you feel relaxed.

3. On the right side of the page, list how often you engage in these activities using the following categories: daily, several times per week, several times per month, once a month, and less than once a month.

4. Notice the patterns of your own antistress behaviors and take note of what behaviors you may want to increase to bring more peace and calm to your life.

ACTION STEP 5.2: Name Your Stressors

For this step, make a chart like the one in the previous action step: divide a blank journal page in half by drawing a line down the middle.

1. Think about various situations in your life that make you feel stressed. These events may include times when you feel rushed in your morning routine, are stuck sitting in rush-hour traffic, feel overcommitted to activities such as the PTA or volunteering in your community or church, are having conflict in your relationship with your partner or children, or are dealing with a fast-paced work environment. On the left-hand side of your journal page, list the top five situations that make you feel stressed.

2. On the right side of the page, list how often you experience these stressful events using the following categories: daily, several times per week, several times per month, once a month, and less than once a month.

3. You can use this information to assess some of the activities you may want to *decrease* or change to keep your stress levels low or reduce the impact of these stressful events on your life. While you may be unable to immediately change some stressful situations, such as sitting in rush-hour traffic or working in a fast-paced environment, you *can* learn to change your reaction to them.

ACTION STEP 5.3: Assess the Impact of Stress on Your Bipolar Disorder

For many people with bipolar disorder, stress triggers symptoms, and if you're already experiencing symptoms, stress may aggravate them, making them worse. However, as you know, bipolar disorder is different for everyone, so this action step will help you explore whether stress is a trigger for you. These questions are more easily applied to single events than daily stressors. Later in this chapter, you'll learn methods of coping with the everyday stress of life. This action step will help you and your mental health provider understand the impact of stress on your behaviors and on your bipolar disorder.

Review your list of your five most stressful situations from the previous action step. For each of the five situations, answer the following questions:

1. On a scale of 0 to 10 (with 0 meaning no symptoms and 10 meaning extreme symptoms), how would you rate the severity of your bipolar symptoms before the stressor occurred?

2. In the two weeks after the stressor occurred, how would you rate the severity of your bipolar symptoms?

3. Did you increase your use of alcohol, cigarettes, drugs, TV, or computers after the stressor?

4. Did your appetite change (ate more or less, or indulged in certain types of food) as a result of this stressor?

5. Were there any other behavioral, emotional, or psychological responses to the stressor?

6. How long did it take you to return to your "normal" self?

Look for linkages between stressors and behaviors. Look at your Weekly Moods and Triggers Chart and see if any of your responses to the questions above are linked to your triggers and moods. You'll want to reduce the triggers by reducing stress, and decrease the likelihood of an episode by increasing the relaxing activities in which you participate. Later you'll learn coping strategies that will reduce the impact of the stressors you can't control.

ACTION STEP 5.4: Reduce Stress in Your Life

For this action step you'll write a plan to eliminate some of your stressful situations, and reduce or change any behaviors that cause stress in your life. Use your loose-leaf binder, because you'll track these activities over time.

At the top of five pages in your binder, write each of the five stressful situations you listed earlier in Action Step 5.2, one per page. You'll make a plan for reducing each of the behaviors that cause stress or your time spent in stressful situations. Make your plans specific and give yourself a time line for achieving your goals and specific objectives that will give you a sense of accomplishment once you've achieved them.

First, set a goal for making a change. For example, if you find that driving in traffic is really stressful for you, you may make it your goal to reduce the stress of driving in your life. At the top of a page, write a goal statement that starts, "I will…," and then complete it in exact terms: "I will make driving less stressful for me." Set a date for achieving your goal. Below that date, make a three-column table with one large column on the left, where you'll list the strategies you'll take to achieve that goal. In the middle column, write the date by which you plan to achieve that goal, and, in the last column, write the date you actually achieve your goal. In this case, a month is a long enough period for changing driving habits. For example, you could decide to take public transit and use the time to read a book or work-related materials. You could continue to drive but listen to relaxing music, an audio book, or a language-instruction CD. You could carpool and use the time to read a book. You could also ask your boss for a slight change in schedule to reduce the impact of traffic on your life. Let your boss know that you'd be more consistently on time if commuting slightly before or after normal commuter periods and that your reduced stress levels would improve your productivity.

At the end of the first week, check your progress so far to assess whether your time line is unrealistic and may require an extension or a switch to another goal. In your binder, use a sheet of paper to write a short progress report summarizing how well you're doing for each of the five plans you made. Now is a good time to redo Action Step 5.2 to monitor your progress. You can also monitor your progress by answering the following questions at the end of each week for a month. Change your goals and objectives based on your evaluation. You may want to focus on other goals or extend your time line for achieving the ones you've already set.

1. Are you feeling less stressed than you were last week? If so, why?

2. Are you feeling more stressed then you were last week? If so, why?

3. Have you implemented any of your stress reduction plans, and if so, what effect have they had on your life?

4. What are some strategies you want to try to further reduce your stress levels?

At the end of the month or any other time frame you've set for yourself, evaluate how you're doing on achieving your goals. You may want to review weekly your progress toward your goal and take concrete steps toward achieving them. In the last example, you could take a comprehensive approach by doing one, two, or all of the suggested strategies. You could simply leave the driving to someone else and take public transit. Or you could combine changing your work schedule with listening to relaxing music when you're driving. Taking at least one step toward your goal on a weekly basis will help you achieve your goal in one month.

Another way to reduce stress in your life includes reducing the amount of time you spend waiting in lines. To achieve this goal you may choose to run your errands when you're likely to find fewer people in line. For example, early-morning or late-evening bank trips make for shorter lines. A Sunday morning grocery trip will reveal a fairly empty store. You may find that you don't usually manage your time well, which forces you to rush to finish tasks right before deadlines. You may choose instead to work daily on tasks, doing a little bit at a time. This is particularly useful for people living with bipolar disorder, because at least some of your work will get done when you're feeling well so that you aren't crunched for time when you're not feeling so well.

Whatever your goals, use one page for each goal, keeping track of the tasks and strategies you'll use to achieve that goal by listing them on the left side of the page and writing the goal date and achievement date on the right side of the table.

EXECUTING YOUR STRESS REDUCTION PLANS

Whatever your situation, make a plan and execute it. Plans can be as simple as getting up fifteen minutes earlier for work so you can eat a real breakfast, read the paper over coffee, or have some quiet time before the rest of your household (or the world) awakes. There's something incredibly pacifying in a sunrise. Or you may choose to use those fifteen minutes to beat the stressful rush-hour traffic. Using the table in Action Step 5.4 to keep track of your progress will help you track how well you're executing your plans to reach your goals.

ACTION STEP 5.5: Increase the Peace in Your Life

This action step helps you look at all the activities in your life that bring you peace and joy, and find ways to increase the amount of time you spend doing them. You'll need a blank page in your binder.

Write the first of the five activities you listed earlier in Action Step 5.1 that bring you peace. Make a plan to increase the amount of time you spend doing that activity. For example, if you like spending time with friends but find you "have no time" to meet with them, phone or e-mail a friend asking him or her to meet with you next week. You may think you have no time, but perhaps you can meet and run errands together, like shopping for groceries or making a trip to the dry cleaners, or maybe you can make a plan to exercise together as a healthy alternative to going out for drinks or coffee. Another way to share time is to trade making dinner at each other's home. You could even meet at a carwash and catch up while your cars are getting cleaned. Try to make this the first of a regular monthly or weekly visit, depending on the circumstance. Explain to your friends that you enjoy their company, have missed seeing them, and would like to plan to see them more often.

Make time for yourself. If one of your peaceful activities is something you enjoy doing alone but you find that family and work obligations interfere with your ability to make that commitment to yourself, you may need to practice giving your own needs top priority sometimes. For example, you may like going for walks but find that, after making dinner for the family and putting the kids to bed, you're just too tired in the evenings to walk. Ask yourself if there are other times in the day when you can take time to walk, for instance, in the morning before the kids are awake or during your lunch hour at the office. Or you may ask your partner, if you have one, to make dinner twice a week and put the kids to bed so you can take an after-dinner walk. It's important to make your own need for relaxation and stress reduction a priority, even if it means saying no to another commitment or asking a loved one to help out.

Improve your mood. Make a plan for increasing the number of activities that improve your mood (review Action Step 5.1). Once you've set this goal, you'll need to decide what actions to take. Are you going to see one friend or two once a month? Will you take a lunchtime walk every workday or three times per week? Setting easily achievable objectives makes it easy to measure your success.

Try to increase the frequency of the stress-reducing activities that bring you peace. If you only do a particular activity once a week, then you may choose to do it twice per week. If you need to, schedule time on your calendar, PDA, or day planner and give yourself at least half an hour, if not more, to do the stress-free activity.

After you've done the activity, write in your journal how it affected your stress level and mood, and notice how long the effect lasts. You may notice that your mood remains improved through the next day as well.

Evaluate your progress. At the end of the first week, check your progress to assess whether you created an unrealistic plan that may require you to extend your time line or change your strategies. In your journal, write a short progress report that summarizes how well you're doing. Ask yourself the four questions in Action Step 5.4.

Adapt your plan. Change your goals and strategies based on your evaluation. If you have trouble implementing your strategies, you may find that you need to take slower, smaller steps toward your objectives and set less ambitious goals for the next week. Or, you may find that it was so easy to implement your new stress-reducing plan that you can now add a new peaceful activity to decrease your stress level even more.

MORE WAYS TO REDUCE STRESS IN YOUR LIFE

It would be great if we had no stress in our lives and all we had to do was wake up on a tropical beach and eat fresh fruit and fish washed down with coconut water, but that's merely a fantasy for 99.9 percent of us. For those of us who live in the real world, stress is a part of our daily lives. Below is a discussion of ways to reduce the impact of stress on your life. You may find some of these techniques a useful addition to the stress reduction activities you discovered in the action steps above.

Be Assertive in Setting Boundaries

If you have difficulty saying no when asked to commit your time or energy, try practicing a simple script, such as "No, thank you. I'm flattered by your request and really wish I could, but I like to do a great job when I participate, and the current demands on my time would make this next to impossible. If I know of anyone who might be interested, I'll refer him or her to you." Try reciting this in front of a mirror or with a friend. Here are some steps for setting boundaries that allow you to control your life and how you spend your time:

1. Pay attention to your physical and emotional reactions. If you feel suffocated, overwhelmed, angry, or resentful at a request for your time, pay attention to that. That's your sign to consider saying no.

2. When you need to set a boundary with someone, state your position firmly and calmly, without anger, and use confident body language (stand up straight, face the person squarely, and look him or her in the eye as you speak).

3. After you have set a boundary, support that boundary by your actions. For example, if you tell your coworker that you can't take on a particular task, don't go back later and offer to do part of the task because you feel guilty at having said no. Stand by your own boundaries.

4. Realize that if you're unused to setting boundaries, you may feel frightened, ashamed, or guilty at first. This is normal, and you'll become more comfortable with boundary setting as you get more practice.

5. Having a supportive friend can be helpful when learning to set boundaries. If you feel comfortable doing so,

engage a friend to be your "boundary-setting buddy" and act as a team in improving your boundary-setting skills.

Exercise Is the Best Medicine for Stress

Exercise is probably the most effective way to manage stress. Exercise gives us energy to deal with stressors while providing an outlet for tension caused by stress. It also increases the natural mood-elevating chemicals in our brains and prepares us to deal with stressors in healthier ways. Often when we're stressed, it's not that we need more time but, rather, more energy. More energy increases our productivity by improving our ability to focus, concentrate, process new information, and elevate our mood. (We'll explore how to start and maintain an exercise regimen in chapter 7.)

Some particularly effective exercises for coping with stress are yoga and walking. Yoga is a calm and relaxing exercise that tones and strengthens our bodies, and gives us strategies for dealing with stress through deep breathing and stretches. Walking is exercise you can do anywhere and anytime; even a few minutes of walking after a stressful event can bring you back to a more centered and calm place. You may want to keep a pair of sneakers or other comfortable shoes in your car or at the office so that you're prepared at any time to take five minutes to get some fresh air, increase your metabolism, burn calories and reduce stress.

Good Nutrition Every Day Keeps Stress Away

Following a balanced diet with lots of fresh fruits and vegetables allows your body to respond to stress in a healthier way. (We'll discuss nutrition in more detail in chapter 8.) Like exercise, good nutrition prevents diseases that could impact our overall health and well-being (whereas chronic illness often causes depression), and can also elevate mood through nutrients such as omega-3 fatty acids.

Get a Good Night's Sleep

Getting a good night's sleep improves your concentration and productivity, and reduces your irritability. When you're well rested, it's much easier to solve problems, and stressful situations often don't seem as frustrating. Just observe children as they get tired; their ability to perform any task or to behave appropriately becomes more challenging the later it gets. Sleep is of particular importance to people living with bipolar disorder and will be explored in the next chapter.

Connect and Engage

For ongoing stress relief, seek support from your family and friends. (We'll explore support systems further in chapter 9.) Having a support system means having someone to talk to when you feel stressed, which can help relieve some of the pent-up feelings that can contribute to stress, such as frustration, anger, and anxiety. Our loved ones may also give us new perspectives that change the way we perceive the source of the stress.

Your support system can also help you manage your daily responsibilities so that you have less to do and more company to do it with. For example, if you have children, you might ask a family member to watch the children so you can go out and see your favorite band in concert or take some time to pamper yourself.

Plan Ahead

Even with the best stress management skills in the world, we'll all have bad days sometimes. Planning ahead for stressful times can help. Especially for people with bipolar disorder, who may have unexpected mood swings with unknown consequences, it can help to make sure work assignments, chores, and other important tasks are done earlier than the deadline in case an episode comes on suddenly. You can also make a habit of maximizing your productivity during times when you're full of energy to make up for the times when you're slogging through the day.

Keeping everything in order and completing tasks early when you have energy helps reduce the impact of unfinished tasks and low energy when your functioning is lower. Planning ahead can reduce the stressor of the unknown and the anxiety that can so easily trigger a manic or depressive episode. Planning ahead also means to schedule time for yourself, your exercise, and your family and friends. We reveal our priorities by how much attention we give to the people and things in our lives, so show how important you are to yourself by scheduling time for you.

Here are some ways you can plan ahead to reduce stress:

- Use online banking to pay your bills as they come in (you can set the date for payment in the future).

- For a work task with a deadline, plan to use one hour per day to work on it so that the bulk of it isn't left for the day or night before the deadline.

- Plan your driving trips to cover as many errands as possible per trip. This not only saves time and stress but reduces your cost for parking and gas. For example, choose a grocery store near a pharmacy, a bank, and a dry cleaner so you can do all these errands in one area.

- Call ahead, which can save you a lot of waiting time. For example, call the dry cleaner to let them know you're coming so you can simply pick up your clothes without waiting for them to search. Program the phone numbers to your favorite take-out places into your cell phone so you can call in your order before you arrive. You can do the same for your favorite coffee place if you plan to have a big order.

- Walk instead of drive. If you live within two miles of where you want to go, you may choose to walk for the exercise rather than deal with the stress of parking and waiting. Call ahead and then put on your walking shoes.

- If your mood starts to get low and you find you don't have the energy to complete your important tasks, consider asking your support system for help to reduce your stress and the severity of an episode before it gets too serious.

Treat Yourself Well

During stressful times, it's particularly important to treat yourself well. Give yourself a treat when you're feeling stressed. For some people it's a home pedicure, and for others it's a professional one. It may mean a long bath, a facial, or a massage. Do whatever makes you feel special and spoiled when you're feeling particularly stressed. As mentioned in the previous section, schedule time for yourself, because your mental health is worth it.

Develop Structure and a Routine

Structure and routine reduce stress because your body goes into automatic pilot. For example, many people are challenged to find their keys when they're ready to leave home. Simply placing a hook near the door on which to hang the keys means one less thing to cause stress if you're running late in the morning. For women, it may mean only changing purses at the end of the week instead of during the week so they can take enough time to transfer all their important items from one purse to another. Finding your cell phone or the handset for your landline is also a common stressor that can be simply solved by returning the handset after all calls and keeping your cell phone in the same place. Routine reduces the anxiety of the new. This doesn't mean that we should never make changes or experience new things, but a daily routine requires less mental energy and means fewer unpleasant surprises and thus less unexpected stress.

Meditate

Meditation is a great strategy for de-stressing in the moment. Sometimes anxiety may build as a result of a stressful event, which is when some meditation strategies may be especially useful. There are many books dedicated to meditation, and one of these books may be a very useful addition to your library.

One of the simplest meditation strategies is to simply focus on your breathing; slow it down and take long, deep breaths through your nose that you blow out through your mouth. Mentally count as you breathe in for five seconds: one-potato, two-potato, and so on until you get to five-potato, then blow out for five seconds, counting the same way (saying "potato" approximates a second). Do this five times and you'll find that your heart rate has slowed down, and you may find it easier to find a solution to the situation at hand. This strategy also reduces the likelihood of anxiety as a result of being stressed. Other times you may retreat to a quiet space and sit quietly, recalling a place and time when you felt most at peace.

Create a Relaxing Environment

Make your surroundings as calming as possible. For example, painting the walls blue will help you feel calm every time you enter a room. You can put pictures of your favorite places on your walls, on your bedside table, or in your wallet or select one as your computer screen saver. Lighting candles is also a great way to reduce stress. Place candles around your home and use them as lighting when you don't need bright lights. Put them in safe spots away from heavy traffic areas or flammable fabrics or plants, and remember to put them out before bedtime or before leaving the house. The warm glow of candles is very relaxing.

Aromatherapy can also help you to de-stress. Chamomile is known for calming the stomach and mind, as are the scents of lavender and ylang ylang. You can buy these items at shops that sell home and bath products. You can keep them in your office, put drops on your pillow, or use them in candle or essential oil form to scent a room or your bathtub. You can also use edible herbs as tea (as in the case of chamomile).

Greenery also helps us relax, which is why it's in the bucolic environments surrounding many mental health care facilities. So get some plants and place them in windowsills or in areas where you'll easily see them. Caring for them and watching them grow and bloom may bring you peace and satisfaction, and provide a relaxing environment. African violets, cacti, spider plants, and geraniums can survive the lack of care that may occur during depressive episodes.

A fish bowl is also a great addition to a relaxing environment. Sometimes the distraction of watching fish swim around is enough to take our minds off our troubles. They're also easy to care for. (Note how many doctors' and dentists' offices have fish.)

Plan a Do-Nothing Day

Have a pajama day, when you spend the day in your pajamas doing nothing but your favorite indoor activities. Turn off the phone and relax with a book, or some knitting or other craft project, or head off into the kitchen to create a simple but tasty dish. This is a conscious act, not surrender to depression. If you feel depressed, please don't do this activity, because you may find yourself in a position that makes it hard to reengage with the world.

Plan a Tune-Out Day

The do-nothing day could be part of your tune-out day and vice versa, when you turn off the phone, TV, computer, and radio. Ignore the newspaper, because everything in it has already happened. We spend so much time taking in information and being bombarded with ideas and thoughts that aren't our own that sometimes we need to turn off the outside noise to hear ourselves and give our brains some time to recover from the stress of the media onslaught.

Plan a Getaway Day

Lastly, one idea that works for many people is getting away from your home or town. You don't need a lot of money or time to get away from your usual surroundings for a day or two. You can spend a day at the beach, hiking in the woods, or at an out-of-town fair. For some, nothing beats being near water or in the woods, and both hit the jackpot. Keep a blanket in the car, and on a nice day just drive to your favorite spot (the less crowded, the better) and sit on your blanket and watch time, waves, or people passing by.

You may know of other things that calm you, and whatever they are, use them when your life gets stressful. A good prevention strategy is to do these enjoyable things even when there is no need. Maintaining mental health is about prevention, not cure. Nevertheless, it's never too late to start.

PSYCHOTHERAPY

Usually, the problem with stress isn't the stressful situation itself but how we react to it. Much research has been done on ways we can change our reactions to stressful events. One successful method is cognitive behavioral therapy (CBT), which can be very useful for changing the way we think about, and react to, the events of our lives. CBT teaches people to pay attention to what they tell themselves about a stressful event and change that internal message, as well as the problematic behavior.

For example, someone who loses a job may feel anxious and stressed because he believes he's a failure and will never again find a job that fits his skills and interests. He may be afraid to look for another job, because he fears the humiliation and painful feelings he'll experience if he applies for a job and doesn't get it. CBT can teach that person to explore, understand, and change the messages he's telling himself about himself; help him see his experience in the broader context of his life; and help him learn and practice new behaviors that decrease his chronic stress, such as better time management techniques for greater success at the next job.

In this chapter you learned that stress has physical, emotional, and psychological impacts on our lives. Stress can trigger or exacerbate a bipolar episode. For those of us with bipolar disorder, understanding how stress triggers episodes gives us some control over our lives by helping us prevent and manage our stress. There are many ways of coping with stress. Stress management requires a change in thinking and behavior. You've completed action steps that helped you identify your major stressors and your preferred ways of coping. You've also been given an extensive list of strategies you can use to try to help minimize the impact of stress and reduce the likelihood of experiencing bipolar disorder symptoms.

CHAPTER 6

Get Enough Sleep

Tuesday, February 17, 2004

Well, mania is upon me. There I was, at 3:30 A.M. sweeping the baseboards … It's so frustrating. I haven't even yawned. I've swept and done laundry, and now it's 4:30 A.M. and I'm doing push-ups and sit-ups.

This is an entry from my own journal, and if you have bipolar disorder and any experience with mania, it may seem familiar to you. Some people wish they had that much energy. And there are times when mania's creative and productive side benefits lure you into the danger of getting no sleep. Trying to manage mania is a very risky endeavor. Eventually the sleep deprivation leads your brain to malfunction in serious ways that can lead to hospitalization, because both lack of sleep (insomnia) and too much sleep can worsen moods.

To people with bipolar disorder, often the possibility of getting regular sleep doesn't seem real. Regular sleep may seem like a pipe dream. But take it from one who knows, it *is* possible. Many people living with bipolar disorder have spent a lifetime going to bed later than everyone else and having a hard time with mornings as a result. Or you may get no sleep at all and feel fine. And even worse, because of the awful feelings of depression, you may sleep all the time. Sleep can be your enemy in many ways. When manic, you may sleep little, and when depressed, you may sleep too much or not at all.

INSOMNIA

The truth is that almost everyone experiences insomnia at some point in his or her life. If it becomes a chronic condition, it can impact your quality of life by negatively affecting your work performance and ability to complete daily tasks, increasing your risk of accidents, and making you irritable.

Causes and Symptoms of Insomnia

The symptoms of insomnia include trouble falling asleep; awakening frequently during the night; awakening very early and being unable to return to sleep; and experiencing fatigue during the day, morning headaches, and irritability (as anyone with a young child knows).

Some of the conditions that can cause sleeplessness include stress, a change in your normal routine, bright lights, too much caffeine or alcohol use, an uncomfortable bed, a snoring roommate or bed partner, moving to a high altitude, and caring for a child or aging parent. Sleep usually returns when the situation returns to normal.

Bipolar Disorder and Insomnia

The irony of the relationship between insomnia and bipolar disorder is that staying up late or going without sleep can cause insomnia (the inability to fall asleep), and lack of sleep can also trigger a bipolar episode, especially a manic or hypomanic episode. People living with bipolar disorder are often sensitive to changes in their internal clocks (circadian rhythms), which regulate sleep. Such changes can be caused by any major change in daily routine or the change of seasons.

Insomnia and Co-occurring Disorders

In addition to bipolar disorder, other mental illnesses (such as anxiety and depression) and mood disorders not only cause insomnia but also are made worse by lack of sleep. Other causes of insomnia include coexisting medical conditions, such as restless legs syndrome, sleep apnea, Parkinson's disease, Alzheimer's disease, and chronic pain from a host of illnesses. Sometimes treating the underlying disorder will reduce or eliminate the insomnia. There are many medicines that also cause insomnia: oral contraceptives, cold medicines, appetite suppressants, decongestants, diuretics, amphetamines, some antidepressants, some tranquilizers, and some drugs prescribed to reduce cholesterol and hypertension.

SLEEP HABITS

Insomnia can also be caused by poor sleep habits, including the following list of behaviors:

- Napping in the daytime

- Excess activity prior to bedtime, such as mental or physical exercise, intense interactions with others, or watching exciting media

- Doing activities in bed other than sleeping, such as watching TV, reading, or writing

- Using alcohol, caffeine, or tobacco close to bedtime

A Regular Sleep-Wake Schedule

People living with bipolar disorder need to maintain a regular sleep-wake schedule (Srinivasan et al. 2006). Routine has been found to be an important factor in preventing recurrence of bipolar disorder symptoms (Frank, Gonzalez, and Fagiolini 2006). Because mania and depression often interrupt sleep, and sleep deficit has been found to be a risk factor or warning sign for future mood episodes (Bauer et al. 2006; Umlauf and Shattell 2005), consistent sleep patterns are an important feature of bipolar symptom management and relapse prevention.

One study found that sleep deficit predicted depressive symptoms, and the authors recommended sleep management as an intervention (Perlman, Johnson, and Mellman 2006). Inadequate or poor-quality sleep has even been found to be a predictor of suicide in people without mental illness (Goodwin and Marusic 2006). As noted above, sleep loss is a very common trigger for mania and hypomania.

ACTION STEP 6.1: Log Your Sleep Time

If you haven't already begun to do so, start keeping track of the number of hours you sleep on the Weekly Moods and Triggers Chart you started in chapter 4; there's a row for sleep in the "Triggers" section. Each morning record the number of hours you slept the night before. This number should reflect the total number of hours you slept, so deduct any time you may have spent awake in the middle of the night. Keep track of your sleep for at least one month or for as long as you use your Weekly Triggers and Moods Chart. (Any time there's a change in your symptoms or medication, resume logging for at least a month to monitor and manage your symptoms and triggers.)

Shifts in sleep patterns may precede or accompany bipolar symptoms, and may indicate the onset of an episode. Tracking your sleep patterns can help your mental health care provider develop a treatment plan that addresses any sleep issues you have. You may also find that, if you sense an episode coming on, monitoring your sleep and taking the appropriate steps to address any insomnia or troubling sleep patterns can mediate or prevent a bipolar episode.

While working on your sleep habits, it's a good idea to keep a more detailed sleep log than simply recording your number of sleep hours on the Weekly Moods and Triggers Chart. The following log is one way of doing this. To complete this action step, you'll need a clock next to your bed. To replicate the sample Weekly Sleep Log, follow the instructions below (or photocopy the following chart for your binder). Fill out the log every morning.

1. Make a table with eight columns (see the column headings in the blank form).

2. Write the day and the date.

3. The first night you start monitoring your sleep, record the time you got into your bed.

4. The next morning record the time you fell asleep the night before. (Make an estimate, because you probably won't accurately know this time within more than fifteen minutes to a half hour.)

5. Then record the number of times you awoke on the previous night. Be sure to keep a pen and your binder by the bed so you can scribble the times of your waking and sleeping episodes during the night.

6. Record the time you awoke to begin your day in the morning.

7. Calculate the number of hours you slept by subtracting all the time you were awake from the time you were asleep.

8. Next, record the quality of your sleep on a scale of 0 to 10, with 0 meaning that you had a peaceful night and 10 representing a night in which you had nightmares, tossed and turned, and woke several times during the night.

If you regularly awaken during the night for any reason at all, talk this over with your health care provider. If your insomnia makes it difficult for you to make it through the day, also discuss this with your health care provider. It may be simply that you take trips to the bathroom because you drink a lot of fluids just before bedtime, or it may be a side effect of your medications. For example, polyuria, or frequent urination, is a side effect of lithium. Once you awaken to go to the bathroom, it may be hard to return to sleep. However, all of this is best discussed with your medical provider so that he or she can assess all the possible factors involved and help you get restful sleep.

Monitoring your sleep is something you'll do on a regular basis with the Weekly Moods and Triggers Chart. However, when you're having sleep difficulties, either too much or too little sleep, you can keep the Weekly Sleep Log to better monitor your sleep, understand the nature of your difficulties, and track your progress in changing your sleep routine (see the following action step).

CHART 6.1: Weekly Sleep Log

Day	Date	Bedtime	Time You Fell Asleep	Number of Times You Awoke	Morning Wake Time	Number of Sleep Hours	Quality of Sleep
Mon							
Tue							
Wed							
Thur							
Fri							
Sat							
Sun							

ACTION STEP 6.2: Eliminate Poor Sleep Habits

Most adults need seven to eight hours of sleep per night, but only you know how much you need. If you wake up feeling rested (and not in a state of mania during which you need little sleep) after seven to eight hours of sleep, then that's how much sleep you need on average. You can use incidence of symptoms to help measure when you're getting too little sleep. However, six hours is a marker for insufficient sleep and thus a good sign that you're not getting enough sleep. This action step is about getting your sleep habits in the healthy range on a regular basis.

If you get fewer than six hours' sleep on any given night, you may be at risk of having a bipolar episode. Review the list of poor sleep habit behaviors and other possible causes of insomnia to see if any relate to your situation. Write down which of these behaviors and causes might be an issue for you and choose one to start changing. Set a goal to change this behavior in one month. Write your goal at the top of a sheet of paper in your binder and note at least three actions you'll take to eliminate this behavior. Divide the rest of the page in two using the first column for the date and the second column for your actions to change this behavior. Each day, write down what action you took to reduce or eliminate this behavior until you no longer have that poor sleep habit. You may then choose another behavior to work on, as applicable.

For example, if you currently watch television in your bedroom at bedtime, you may want to start reducing the amount of time you watch it by fifteen minutes each night for one week. The second week you may decide to remove the TV from the bedroom. Because you'll want to make sure you don't fall asleep in front of the TV once it's moved to another room, your next step may be to set a regular bedtime, when you'll go to your bedroom and get into bed. Track your success until you start doing this on a regular basis. This will help you eliminate the habit of watching TV in your bedroom and falling asleep in front of it.

You may find it helpful to discuss these behaviors or causes with your mental health care provider, who may provide solutions to your sleep problems that may be as simple as reducing your intake of caffeine in the afternoon or eliminating alcohol in the evening. If you're sleeping more than nine hours on a regular basis (on more than one night per week) without being physically ill, you might want to also discuss this with your medical provider to explore the possible sources of this issue, which could include depression or overuse of sleep medications.

TREATMENT FOR INSOMNIA

The main treatments for insomnia include behavioral programs, medications (over-the-counter, prescription, and herbal), and improved sleep hygiene. Without going into detail, some of the behavioral programs include cognitive behavioral therapy (CBT; discussed in chapter 2) and relaxation and meditation strategies. Medications used for sleep include the family of drugs related to benzodiazepines, such as Ambien (zolpidem), Halcion (triazolam), Sonata (zaleplon), and Lunesta (eszopiclone); antidepressants, such as Desyrel (trazodone) or Remeron (mirtazapine); and some antipsychotic medications, such as Seroquel (quetiapine), because of their sedating qualities.

The easiest place to start treating insomnia is to change your sleep-related behavior. If your strategies don't work, discuss other interventions with your provider. This chapter focuses on the behaviors you can control, action strategies that will give you the necessary positive reinforcement to take control and change your life.

GOOD SLEEP HABITS

Good sleep habits include the following activities that promote falling asleep, staying asleep, and waking up feeling rested in the morning:

- Go to bed only when sleepy (except if you are having an episode of mania).

- Establish a good sleep environment: a dark bedroom with limited distractions (low noise, dim light, and cool temperature). Use a sleeping mask or blindfold if necessary.

- Avoid foods, beverages, and over-the-counter medications that may contain stimulants, such as caffeine.

- Avoid alcohol and nicotine at least two hours before bedtime.

- Decrease or eliminate caffeine consumption (including chocolate and green tea). If at all possible, take no caffeine after noon.

- Exercise regularly, around midday or early afternoon (but not in the evening).

- Use behavioral and relaxation techniques to facilitate physical and mental relaxation. These can include deep breathing and meditation (see chapter 5).

- Avoid naps in the late afternoon or evening.

- Avoid heavy meals close to bedtime.

- Get into the habit of doing a relaxing activity at least an hour before bedtime, such as reading, sewing, knitting, making models, and watching TV.

- Avoid protein snacks in the evening (for example, cheese or nuts).

- Avoid drinking fluids right before bedtime. This may present a problem for people who have dehydration as a medication side effect. Although taking fluids at bedtime may cause you to have to get up and empty your bladder during the night, the cost of not having enough fluids could be toxicity or other problematic side effects, such as dry mouth, which may discourage you from taking your medications.

- Use the bed only for sleep and intimacy. (Don't eat, read, use your laptop, or watch TV in bed.)

■ Keep your room cool, because cooler body temperatures are associated with more time spent in deep sleep.

■ Establish a regular wake-time schedule. This is a high-yield strategy. It's important to awaken at the same time every day (weekdays and weekends) and preferably expose yourself to bright light upon awakening (for example, open the drapes and shutters to let sunlight into your room). This routine has been shown to be a powerful way to regulate the circadian rhythm, which is important for maintaining mood stability (Jones 2001).

If none of these sleeping tricks works for you, spend no longer than fifteen minutes awake in bed before arising to do something else, and return later to try to get back to sleep.

The goal of maintaining good sleep habits is to associate the bed and the bedroom with sleep, and to condition your mind to sleep once you get into your bed. Following the guidelines above can go a long way in fighting your sleep demons and helping you get a good night's sleep on a regular basis.

If you work afternoon or overnight shifts, you can use these strategies to help your body develop a routine that accommodates your work hours. Many people who do shift work are less likely to get enough sleep and often suffer from fatigue. People with bipolar disorder need to decrease the likelihood of fatigue, because it can trigger episodes. Furthermore, if possible, minimize fluctuations in your sleep routine, because shifts in your schedule may trigger bipolar episodes. Good sleep habits are of supreme importance when you have to sleep while others are awake. The cooperation of your housemates or family in supporting routine and restful sleep will go a long way in helping you achieve your sleep goals. You may have to try harder to have a dark, quiet space, but it will be worth it.

ACTION STEP 6.3: Adopt Healthy Sleep Habits

Review the good sleep habit strategies above, note the ones you currently practice, and continue practicing them. Of those you don't practice, choose one good sleep habit to add to your repertoire each week for the next month. For each, monitor your implementation on a page in your binder. Write each behavior on the top of a page, and then write two or three ways to incorporate this behavior into your life. On the rest of the page, keep a daily journal of your progress. For example, if you practice meditation to get more relaxed so you can sleep better, write that down each day and use the Weekly Sleep Log in Action Step 6.1 to monitor the impact of this behavior change on your sleep. If you choose to avoid heavy meals late in the evening, you may want to track the times you have dinner every evening until you achieve your goal, which may be sticking to a specific mealtime of 6:00 P.M. or eating an hour earlier than usual. When you change your sleep-related behaviors, track your progress on a Weekly Sleep Log for at least one week or until you achieve your behavioral goal.

For example, if you want to avoid heavy meals late in the evening, you may make a list of actions that includes preparing several dinners at a time so that, if you come home late, you don't have to eat dinner late because it will be easy to prepare. You may plan to order in on days you come home late or program the phone numbers of some of your favorite take-out spots into your cell phone so you can call easily and quickly, and pick up your meal on your way home. You may choose to eat a lighter meal if you run late. Lastly, if you usually snack in the late afternoon, you may want to stop so you're ready for dinner earlier in the evening. You may choose to take one or all of these actions, as well as some that you come up with, and log your progress daily until you've adopted some healthier sleep habits into your daily routine.

RELAXING BEFORE BEDTIME

Following the guidelines above really works. If there's something you do that relaxes you, such as reading, sewing, knitting, making models, or watching TV, start that activity about an hour before bedtime. Keep your room dark and cool, because cool rooms promote quicker and deeper sleep. Some people find that lighting candles helps them calm down, so consider lighting some candles in the room where you spend the most time before going to your bedroom. You may use fragrance for relaxation, such as lavender, which has a calming effect. Lighting a lavender- or vanilla-scented candle before doing the dishes, reading a book, or watching TV will help relax you before you retire to your bedroom. As you get ready for bed, dim the lights to calm your senses. Taking a scented bath may also be a great way to wind down after a stressful day.

Sometimes the stresses of the day keep our minds occupied, making it difficult to fall or stay asleep. Make peace with your day so you won't have a lot of thoughts in your head to keep you from sleeping. If thoughts or worries go through your mind and interfere with sleep, try this effective technique: keep your journal by your bedside and write down the bothersome thoughts. This may seem an odd thing to do, but it often works for turning off worrisome thoughts, because you then know you'll remember them later and deal with them some other time.

SLEEP MEDICATIONS

Despite all your best efforts, you may still have difficulty falling or staying asleep, and your provider may suggest taking sleep medications that will not only help you fall asleep but also help you stay asleep. Taking sleep medications is a preventive measure against bipolar episodes caused by sleep irregularities, and it reduces daytime drowsiness or irritation from lack of restful sleep. Your Weekly Sleep Log and Weekly Moods and Triggers Chart will help you and your medical provider choose the medication that's best for you. When you begin taking a sleep medication, or if changes are made in your sleep medications, keep both charts for at least one month after starting the new medication regimen.

Taking your prescribed sleep-inducing medications at your goal bedtime may be too late for them to take effect. Instead, after discussing this with your medical provider, you may want to take them about one to two hours before bedtime to give them time to take effect. Avoid over-the-counter sleep medications unless your medical provider recommends them and monitors your use of them, because they may interrupt your natural sleep routine or interact with other medications you're taking. You can take your sleep medications with sleep-inducing herbal tea, such as chamomile, or tepid water to assist in digesting them. This can become a regular part of your medication routine before bedtime.

Sleep is a major issue for people living with bipolar disorder, because changes in sleep habits may trigger a bipolar episode. Lots of people experience insomnia, because it's caused by many factors, including co-occuring conditions and certain medications and behaviors. Insomnia is both a cause and symptom of bipolar disorder, because you can have trouble falling asleep when depressed and need little sleep when manic, but it can be treated with changes in behavior, psychotherapy, or medications. Good sleep habits promote healthy sleep patterns and reduce the frequency and intensity of bipolar episodes.

CHAPTER 7

Get Regular Exercise

You don't have to be a professional athlete to get the benefits of exercise, which include maintaining a healthy weight, improving heart and lung function, enhancing mood, reducing stress, strengthening your immune system, and improving mental functioning. What's not to love about it? Regular exercise has multiple benefits for everyone, regardless of mental or physical state. Remember, before starting any exercise program, you should consult with your medical care provider to avoid putting your health at risk. You need to work within your body's limitations and strengths.

EXERCISE AND BIPOLAR DISORDER

As mentioned, exercise has many benefits for everyone, especially for people living with mood disorders. Exercise increases cognitive functioning, fights depression, and improves overall mental health (Williams and Strean 2006), because exercise releases many brain chemicals that foster feelings of emotional and psychological well-being. One analysis of many studies found a strong link between weight gain and bipolar disorder (Keck and McElroy 2003). Other researchers found that exercise helps counteract the weight gain that's a side effect of many medications for treating bipolar disorder (McDevitt and Wilbur 2006).

For those of us living with bipolar disorder, exercise not only increases the length and quality of sleep but also has a positive impact on depressive symptoms and takes the edge off mania. Another literature review found that patients with mood disorders have an increased risk for type 2 diabetes and that some atypical antipsychotics, such as Zyprexa (olanzapine), increase risk for diabetes and weight gain (Poulin et al. 2005). Exercise could stave off some of these symptoms related to both the disorder and the medications. However, the ups and downs of bipolar disorder sometimes interfere with our best intentions to keep on track with an exercise program.

How much you move your body often signifies your mood. For example, you may be more active when hypomanic or manic, and less likely to move when depressed. If you make moving your body a part of your daily routine, you may find that, even when you're depressed, exercise may be the one thing you complete that day, which is at least one thing you can feel good about. When you're manic, exercise will take the edge off, release some of your excess energy, and help you concentrate.

EXERCISE AND DEPRESSION

When you're depressed is when you need exercise the most, but it's also the time you least feel like doing anything. If depressed, you may not spend much time moving at all, but the goal is to start by adding a little every day. It may feel like a workout just to get out of bed in the morning, but making it a habit like brushing your teeth will make it easier for you to maintain a program of activity, no matter how depressed you are. You may have been more active before your depression, but doing something is better than nothing. It may be very difficult to start moving, but it will ultimately improve your mood and make you healthier as it boosts your immune system, which gets weakened by depression. Even when sitting on the couch, you can do leg raises, or you can walk the hallway of your apartment or home, or the stairs in your building if you don't want to face the world. Whatever exercise you do, it's better than just sitting or lying there.

One way to increase the likelihood of continuing or beginning an exercise program when you're depressed is to get an exercise buddy or two, or if you can afford one, an exercise trainer. Having people to exercise with gives you a sense of responsibility, not only to yourself but also to others who expect you to show up. You may choose to give them permission to call you if you don't show up or to call you every morning to make sure you show up. Giving a personal trainer permission to call you an hour before exercise time would encourage you to continue. If you have a dog, taking your dog for a walk will get you out of the house for at least a few minutes each day.

EXERCISE AND MANIA

Mania or hypomania can make you feel really energized even if you're irritable, so you'll want activities that will burn off some of that energy and reduce any edginess you feel as a result of your manic symptoms. Now's the time to burn some calories. Make sure to eat if you tend to lose your appetite when having manic symptoms. It may be a good idea to avoid making any decisions about your exercise program when you're experiencing manic or hypomanic symptoms because of the risk of making decisions about purchasing new equipment, clothing, or a gym membership that you may not use. You could let your exercise buddy know about your symptoms and have him or her keep you in check regarding buying equipment and so on.

HOW DO YOU FEEL ABOUT EXERCISE?

Some people read or hear the word "exercise" and conjure up visions of sweaty gyms, groups of people in body-clinging outfits, or a yoga mat with people twisted into seemingly impossible positions. Others think of having to buy equipment and gear, such as new running shoes or weights. However, for our purposes, exercise simply means regular physical activity or movement, and the goal of this chapter is to start you moving and keep you moving.

Our goal is not fitness, but fitness will be a by-product of increased activity. Although there's no workout plan, there's an activity plan for getting the benefits of an active lifestyle—a term that may make you think of hard-core gym rats—but an active lifestyle means one spent moving versus sitting or sleeping. Something is better than nothing. You don't need to be an athlete to reap the physical, psychological, or emotional benefits of regular body movement.

ACTION STEP 7.1: The Positives and Negatives of Exercise

Using the chart below (or a page in your binder), write down five positive words and five negative words that you associate with exercise. See the example at the top of each section.

Positive Words	Reason
Example: *Fun*	*I like swimming.*
1.	
2.	
3.	
4.	
5.	

Negative Words	Reason
Example: *Boring*	*I hate the monotony of swimming or using the stationary bike.*
1.	
2.	
3.	
4.	
5.	

Look at those words, and for each one, write down the reason you feel this way. Understanding why you have negative or positive feelings about exercise will help you plan a physical activity routine that you can maintain. You'll know why you feel good about it (hopefully there was something good on your list) and the source of your negative feelings. These are the areas you'll need to address to get, and keep, you off the couch, bed, or chair. Using the chart below, for each negative feeling, think of a way that you can create a more positive feeling.

For each positive word, think of ways to get more of that positive feeling. There's an example at the top of each section in the chart below. The way to maintain an exercise program is to use the activities in the right-hand column to keep you on track and provide strategies that will keep you moving when you'd rather lie in bed. Every time you notice yourself thinking a negative thought about exercise, consider the positive aspects and you'll stay motivated. Use the strategies in the right-hand column as guidelines for designing your movement program and increasing your activity level to become physically, emotionally, and psychologically healthier than when you started reading this book.

Positive Words	Increase Positive Feelings About Exercise
Example: *Fun*	*Do more exercises I like; do them with my friends.*
1.	
2.	
3.	
4.	
5.	
Negative Words	**Decrease Negative Feelings About Exercise**
Example: *Boring*	*Do things that interest me, such as kayaking, swimming, bike riding, or hiking.*
1.	

2.	
3.	
4.	
5.	

Before you start using the tips in this chapter, write the five positive words on sticky notes and post them in various places in your home where you'll see them every day. They'll affirm your positive feelings toward exercise and reinforce your decision to increase your activity level and manage your symptoms through the benefits that exercise brings. Possible locations include your refrigerator, bathroom mirror, closet door, computer screen, and daily calendar.

HOW MUCH EXERCISE IS ENOUGH?

The surgeon general's report *Physical Activity and Health* (U.S. Department of Health and Human Services 1999) recommends that all adults "accumulate" (which means not necessarily all at once) thirty minutes of moderate intensity activity on most, if not all, days of the week to maintain a healthy level of fitness. "Moderate intensity" means warm and slightly out of breath; you could still carry on a conversation. Losing weight may require longer, more intense exercise. This chapter aims not to shame you for what you aren't doing but, rather, to give you the benefits of exercise through a self-designed program that best suits your likes, dislikes, budget, location, and lifestyle.

ACTION STEP 7.2: Track Your Activity Level

For this action step you'll write down how much time you spend moving every day for the next week. Use a separate page in your binder to keep track of how much exercise you already do and how much you'll do in the future. Alternatively, you can make a table using graph or regular paper, or a computer. You only need to track your exercise for one month to get into the habit. Once you have a steady routine, use your Weekly Moods and Triggers Chart to track whether or not you got enough exercise for the day. Your table will have three columns as in the following example.

SAMPLE TABLE 7.2: Track Your Activity Level

Date	Activity	Duration
June 7	Walked the length of the mall	1 hour
June 7	Walked to the car in parking lot	10 minutes
Daily Total		70 minutes

Here's a blank table you can photocopy. Make enough copies to track your exercise daily for one month, and keep them in your binder.

TABLE 7.2: Track Your Activity Level

	Activity Log	
Date	Activity	Duration
Daily Total		

Add up the total for each day and then total the number of minutes you spent exercising for the entire week. You may be surprised at how much exercise you already do. Or you may realize that you don't move your body enough. The rest of the chapter will help you get the exercise you need without drastically changing your lifestyle all at once. You'll use the log you've kept for one month to measure your progress as you go through the chapter and learn steps for increasing your activity level. By taking gradual steps, you'll build to an activity level that keeps you healthy and improves your mood.

Are You Getting Enough Exercise?

Look at your exercise log for the past week and the totals for each day. Take stock of how your activity level compares to the recommended level. If you're already putting in the right amount of time to exercise, you may choose to simply keep doing what you're doing or increase the number of minutes so you can meet other goals, such as a better fitness level or weight loss. An hour of exercise per day will help you lose weight. If you're not getting enough exercise, the remaining action steps in this chapter will help you develop a plan that works for you. Most people walk every day without thinking of it as exercise, but the amount of steps you take each day counts as exercise that helps keep your mood stable and your heart and lungs happy.

Many sources consider a daily total of ten thousand steps (about five miles) a day an active lifestyle. Two to three thousand steps is considered a sedentary lifestyle. Moving six thousand steps or more per day lengthens your life span, and eight to ten thousand steps per day helps you lose weight (Choi et al. 2007). If you're below the magic number of ten thousand, slowly increase your activity level by perhaps a thousand steps per week until you reach your goal. Remember to check with your medical provider before starting any new exercise program.

ACTION STEP 7.3: Take It Step-by-Step

The best way to measure the number of steps you take in a day is to use a pedometer. You can get a good one for between ten and twenty dollars at fitness specialty stores, major online outlets, and major department stores. Once you have your pedometer, wear it all day every day to keep track of the number of steps you take each day. Instead of a structured exercise program, you can use the guidelines for the number of steps to take per day and find ways to meet that goal. Log that goal in your exercise journal or simply put an *x* in the exercise section on your Weekly Moods and Triggers Chart once you've met the minimum you've set for yourself that day, and then write how many steps you've taken at the end of each day on your Activity Log from the previous action step.

Keeping all your journals and charts in one place will make it easier for you to see how you're doing. For some, it might be easier to use a wall calendar to record how many steps you took on a given day. If you're so inclined, enter the info into a spreadsheet at each month's end and graph your progress over time. It may help to track your number of steps for one month when you begin the exercise program, or for a random week every three months to see if you're still on track, and then make any necessary adjustments to get you at a healthy activity level.

DESIGNING YOUR EXERCISE PROGRAM

The hardest part for many people is choosing an exercise that they would love to do come rain, shine, heat, or cold. You may decide to exercise indoors so that weather's not a factor, but other people find that being outside boosts the benefits. If you love the arts or tourist sites in your town, you could give daily walking tours (as a paid employee or a volunteer). What kind of exercise is best? Whatever physical activity you like to do is the one that's best for *you*. There's no one "best" for everyone, because if you hate the exercise, you won't maintain your program.

Whatever you choose to do, get moving and keep moving. Tracking your daily activity level in steps is an easy way to keep track of your total activity for the day. One minute of bicycling or swimming is the equivalent of 150 steps. Or you may decide to keep track in minutes. Whatever method you choose, make an Activity Log; a small notebook may be the best choice. Many fitness stores offer logs, and several websites have walking logs available as free downloads. Or photocopy the one provided in Action Step 7.2.

ACTION STEP 7.4: Create Your Exercise Program

What Do You Like to Do?

List the types of activities you like to do:

1. _____

2. _____

3. _____

4. _____

5. _____

The Where and How of Your Exercise Plan

1. Using the five activities you listed above and the table below, you'll build an exercise program that works for you. For each of the five activities, list the place where you'd prefer to do it in the second column of the following chart. For example, if you chose walking, you may want to do it at the nearby mall, around a field, around a lake, or on a treadmill at home or the gym.

2. For each of the five activities, list the equipment or gear you'll need for it in the third column.

3. Go through your closet or storage area to see what gear or equipment you already have and list it in

the appropriate column. This includes skis, a tennis racquet, sneakers, a bicycle, and so on.

4. Compare the third and fourth columns of the table to see what items you still need to do your five activities, and list them in the right-hand column.

5. The three activities with the least expensive list of items associated with them will form the basis for your exercise routine. If your program costs too much to maintain, you'll stop doing it, and you don't want cost to stop you from being healthy. It's also best to start with what you already have so you can start right away rather than commit to buying new gear before really committing to a program. If you do buy gear, buy it used at a thrift store so you can minimize your cash layout.

List the three activities that will be the focus of your new exercise program:

1. _____

2. _____

3. _____

Now that you have developed an exercise plan, consult with your medical provider before beginning. Then use the Activity Log from Action Step 7.2 to track your progress.

TABLE 7.4: Create Your Exercise Program

Activity	Place	Gear Needed	Already Own (check)	Cost to Buy
Ex.: *Walking*	*Park*	*Comfy shoes*	√	*Nothing*
1.				
2.				
3.				
4.				
5.				

ACTION STEP 7.5: Fit Exercise into Your Life

Next, you'll list the times of day when you can increase your activity level. Because many people often say that lack of time is the biggest reason for their lack of exercise, think of things you could do later or not at all so you can place your need for exercise higher on your priority list. The things we do reflect our priorities. Get your family to pitch in on chores so you can have more time to get healthy. Take your young child along and set a positive example (carrying a baby in a sling or backpack greatly improves the outcome of any exercise program). Instead of having sedentary meetings, go for a walk together. The next section, Increasing Your Activity Level, provides many ways to integrate movement into your life. To find the times when you're available to exercise, use the table on the following page.

The time ranges you entered into the "Time" column are when you'll do the exercises you like to do. For example, while a swim may be inconvenient in the middle of the day, a fifteen-minute walk may be feasible. You may choose to bike or walk to work, depending on the distance. The next section provides tips for increasing your activity level that you can use in conjunction with the table you just created.

TABLE 7.5: Fit Exercise Into Your Life

Day	Time	Activity
Sunday	*10:00 a.m.-noon* *2:00-4:00 p.m.*	*Taking a walking tour of various art galleries*
Monday	*Lunchtime*	*Walk*
Sunday		
Monday		
Tuesday		
Wednesday		
Thursday		
Friday		
Saturday		

INCREASING YOUR ACTIVITY LEVEL

Because of our on-the-go lifestyle in the United States, it's difficult for most people to schedule regular exercise, which is part of why our country struggles with high rates of obesity and related illnesses, such as diabetes, heart disease, and hypertension.

Most of us could easily increase our activity level simply by increasing the number of steps we take per day. Some people like to swim, hike, bike, play tennis, or do a host of other physical activities. The way to increase your activity level if you're already doing something is to do your favorite activities *more often* or for *longer durations* than you're doing them now. Let's use walking as an example since it's something you don't have to buy special clothes or shoes for. Walking is how we get from place to place, so it's a good starting point for most people unless health problems prevent it, in which case you'd need to consult your doctor to develop a specialized activity program that meets your needs.

Strategies for Increasing Your Activity Level

Below are some ways to increase your activity level. Put a check in the box beside each strategy you think will work for you and try it for a week to see how it goes. If it doesn't work for you, try something else. The goal is to find a routine and stick with it.

☐   Park your car farther from the door when running errands, going shopping, or visiting friends.

☐ Take the stairs instead of the elevator.

☐ Take a dance class or use an exercise video or DVD.

☐ Go dancing with friends.

☐ Take your dog for longer walks.

☐ Get off the bus a stop or two before your destination.

☐ Do some stretches and walking during the commercial breaks of your favorite TV show.

☐ At work, use the most out-of-the-way bathroom, copier, or fax machine.

☐ Deliver items to coworkers instead of sending them through interoffice mail.

☐ While your child plays soccer, walk around the field.

☐ Forget about the drive-through window. Park the car and walk into the building.

☐ Take a ten- to fifteen-minute walk during your breaks and at lunchtime at work. Your productivity will actually increase, because exercise improves brain performance. This will also reduce stress and give your body a break from its routine.

☐ Take walking dates with your loved ones instead of sitting down with a glass of wine or a cup of tea or coffee.

☐ Do errands on foot or bicycle.

☐ Pursue your hobbies by going to trade shows, which often require a lot of walking.

☐ Take a hike. This doesn't require going to the mountains. Simply walk through a park or take an urban hike by finding a route in town and taking a brisk walk along that route.

☐ Take a walking tour of various art galleries.

☐ Get rid of the remote control and walk up to the TV to adjust the volume, change channels, or turn it on or off.

☐ Join an activity club that reflects your own interests. The social aspects and having organized activities you love provide social support and activity. Examples include hiking clubs, swimming clubs, a golfing group, and an outdoor club.

ACTION STEP 7.6: Make an Activity Plan

Using the table in the previous action step, the list you made of the activities you like to do, and the strategies above, complete the following chart to document what activities you plan to do during the next week.

TABLE 7.6: Making an Activity Plan

		Weekly Activity Plan	
Day	Time	Activity	Location
Sunday	*10:00 a.m.–noon* *2:00–4:00 p.m.*	*Take a walking tour of various art galleries*	*Downtown*
Monday	*Lunchtime*	*Walk*	*The park*
Sunday			
Monday			
Tuesday			
Wednesday			
Thursday			
Friday			
Saturday			

BEGINNING YOUR PROGRAM

According to some experts (Leitzmann et al. 2007), the ideal exercise program consists of at least a half hour a day of exercising to the point where your heart rate is up and you feel tired but can still hold a conversation. The key is to start slowly. No matter what activity you choose to start with from the top three list you made in Action Step 7.4, be patient with yourself and don't push yourself to do too much at once. If you choose to walk more, walk for five minutes the first week and then add a minute each day until you reach your ideal amount. If you decide to ride a bicycle or go in-line skating, you may choose to add distance instead of time. However you choose to do it, move slowly until you get to, and possibly even exceed, your exercise goal.

Do something, anything, for a half hour, five to seven days a week. A walk with a friend is a great way to start or break up the day. Use your lunchtime to take a walk; you can eat when you return. You may also find that your stress level at work decreases and you're more alert to finish the day. Swimming can be very relaxing, because of the primal experience of being in water and the minimal level of stress on your joints.

If you're inclined to do more strenuous exercise, then a run or a gym workout may be more to your liking. (Also remember that your local community center may have low-cost exercise programs and equipment that can save you a fortune in gym fees.) The mood boost and weight loss (or maintenance) will have a significant impact on your mental well-being. If you hate gyms or don't want to walk outside, exercise while watching TV. Do stretches, high-knee marching, and strength exercises, such as push-ups, squats, or weight lifting. You'll feel better right away. Just do something, and do it often and for consistent durations.

ACTION STEP 7.7: Get Moving

Choose the date when you'll start your new life of movement. The best day is *today*. The good thing about using a pedometer is that, unless you lie in bed the whole day, you'll record some level of activity. This will give you some positive feedback and encourage you to do more, because you'll find that you actually are active every day. However, the goal is to increase your level of activity to meet or exceed the surgeon general's guidelines of 10,000 steps per day or thirty minutes a day five to seven days a week.

At the end of each day, record your exercise in your Activity Log (see Action Step 7.2) or exercise journal. Check the exercise box on your Weekly Moods and Triggers Chart and also record your mood. Seeing how exercise influences your mood will help you see its significance in your life. Also, making notes in your exercise log about how you feel about your activity for each day will help you keep track of what activities you like and dislike. Do fewer activities you dislike and more of those you do like, which will keep you engaged with your program and reduce the likelihood of stopping.

Case Example: *Karen*

Karen lived near a lake and often took her dog for a short walk so he could get exercise, but she never thought about the exercise she could get if she gave the dog more of a workout. She decided to invite her friend Leyla, whom she hadn't seen in a while, to join her and to bring her dog too. This was so much fun that Karen and Leyla invited several more friends who were trying to live healthier lifestyles, and they now regularly walk around the lake three or four times a week. They bring water bottles and some bring their children along.

Within three months Karen had lost ten pounds and now feels better about herself and more connected to her friends. This has also given her the support she always needed when she felt down and decreased her irritability when she felt manic. As she has learned from noticing the changes recorded in her Weekly Moods and Triggers Chart, she feels better when she exercises. Knowing this gets her out walking even when she feels too depressed to want to go. She also made an agreement with her friends that she'd tell them when she was having symptoms so they'd call her to make sure she made it to the lake. The lesson from Karen's story is this: exercise that involves what we like to do, with people we like, is self-reinforcing, because as our moods improve from exercise, our desire to exercise increases so that we can continue to feel good.

Now that you have a plan based on the kinds of exercise you like to do and the times you have available to do them, before going to bed tonight, get all the things you need ready to start your movement plan tomorrow, the next day, or whatever day you've deemed feasible to start. Of course, *today* is always the best day. Once you have everything you need, you're ready to go.

You don't need to be an athlete to gain the physical, psychological, or emotional benefits of exercise. *All* adults should accumulate thirty minutes of moderate intensity activity on most, if not all, days of the week. Regular exercise has multiple benefits for everyone, regardless of mental state, including lower risk for heart disease, hypertension, and diabetes and improved joint and muscular functioning. Exercise improves your mood and brain function, and helps you get enough sleep. Also, a routine exercise program can minimize the weight-gain side effects of some bipolar medications.

CHAPTER 8

Get Good Nutrition and Take the Right Supplements

As the saying goes, you are what you eat. If you eat junk, you'll have a body that's short on the nutrients it needs to do its daily tasks. Due to your mental illness, you need to eat foods that are high in nutrients and nourish your brain, maximize its functions, and improve your mood. To maintain ideal health, it helps to eat the right combinations of minerals, amino acids, fatty acids, vitamins, fiber, and protein. Eating healthfully gives your body what it needs to create the energy on which you depend to complete your daily activities. For those of us living with bipolar disorder, specific nutrients have been found to help our moods, while other substances, such as alcohol and caffeine, disturb our moods. Although good nutrition is important to everyone's health, if you have bipolar disorder, you may find it helpful to be aware of how, what, when, how much, and why you eat and how this affects your moods.

BIPOLAR DISORDER AND WEIGHT

People living with bipolar disorder have a higher incidence of obesity than the general population, which is linked with physical illnesses and poor mental health outcomes (Wildes, Marcus, and Fagiolini 2006). A study of veterans with bipolar disorder reported that patients with bipolar disorder were more likely to have poor exercise and eating habits than those without the disorder (Kilbourne et al. 2007), and slight changes in exercise and eating habits have recently been found to reduce the impact of Zyprexa on weight gain (Milano et al. 2007). If you decide that you want to lose weight, first consult your medical provider and use a weight loss plan based on a healthy diet and exercise. Skipping meals or eliminating certain foods from your diet may negatively affect your mood or react negatively with your medications.

Eating disorders may also interfere with your treatment, so if you find that you want to severely restrict your diet, vomit after meals, or eat large amounts of food in one sitting, share this information with your mental health care provider so he or she can assist you in getting the appropriate treatment for these unhealthy eating habits.

THE IMPORTANCE OF STAYING HYDRATED

Drinking plenty of water is particularly important for those of us with bipolar disorder, because many of the medications we take cause side effects, such as dry mouth or dehydration, which result from frequent trips to the bathroom. So, it's necessary to drink enough water to stay hydrated and minimize such side effects. One way to ensure getting enough fluids is to drink enough to avoid feeling thirsty during the day. Later, this chapter discusses strategies for giving your body what it needs so you can be healthy and enjoy the things you like to do.

MOOD-ALTERING FOODS

Sugar, caffeine (found in chocolate, coffee, and some teas, such as green and black teas), alcohol, and chocolate have been shown to influence mood (Goldstein, Velyvis, and Parikh 2006). These substances influence brain chemistry in ways that may trigger a bipolar episode. They may also interact negatively with any medications you may be taking. This doesn't mean that you never get to have these things again, but have them in moderation and monitor your intake so you can see what effect, if any, they have on your symptoms. Everyone is different, and alcohol or coffee may have a greater impact on one person's mood than another's. However, substances like alcohol must be avoided when taking certain medications, and this will be marked on the medication container. Strictly follow any directions to avoid certain substances while taking a particular medication so you can avoid negative interactions that could impact your general health, as well as your mood. Certain foods, such as oil-rich fish, fruit, vegetables, and whole grains, may help keep your mood stable. There is some evidence that the B vitamins, zinc, and vitamin C also help stabilize moods (Kaplan et al. 2007).

A HEALTHY DIET

A diet filled with lots of fresh fruits and vegetables in a variety of colors (the more colors, the wider range of nutrients), and adequate protein and carbohydrates goes a long way in keeping you healthy by giving you the nutrients, energy, and fiber your body and brain need to work effectively and efficiently. Eating several small meals per day at the same time each day keeps your blood sugar stable. It's important not to skip meals even if you have no appetite, because this may interfere with the effects of your medication and negatively affect your mood.

FAT AND HEALTH

To maintain a healthy diet, you'll need to monitor your intake of fat, cholesterol, sugars, and salt. Not all fats are bad; some are necessary for your health because they protect organ function and keep hair and skin healthy, and some, such as omega-3 fatty acids, actually improve mood. Omega-3 fatty acids also decrease the risk of coronary artery disease, protect against irregular heartbeat, and help lower blood pressure levels. However, too much fat can be harmful, particularly trans fats or saturated fats, which can increase your bad cholesterol, or LDL (low-density lipoprotein), levels and risk of heart disease. Healthy fats are unsaturated fats, which can lower your risk of heart disease and your LDL levels. (Omega-3s are unsaturated fats.) Some good sources of unsaturated fats are olive, peanut, canola, corn, safflower, and soy oils. Excellent sources of omega-3s are flaxseed and fatty cold-water fish, such as salmon, mackerel, and herring (American Heart Association 2008). However, regardless of the type of fat, too much fat will increase your weight and put you at risk of obesity, which brings other health risks.

Omega-3 Fats and Mood

Omega-3 polyunsaturated fatty acids have been found to positively affect mood in people living with bipolar disorder (Parker et al. 2006), which may mean that a deficit in these biochemicals is related to the onset of depressive episodes. Furthermore, omega-3 supplements are more effective with depressive symptoms than with mania, because they elevate mood (Chiu et al. 2005). Although the studies in this area are in the early stages, the research suggests that omega-3 fatty acids might be an effective part of a comprehensive treatment plan for bipolar disorder. Findings from this newest research reinforce the benefits of omega-3 fatty acids for people living with mood disorders. Some of the best sources of omega-3 fatty acids include fish, such as mackerel, sardines, herring, and salmon, as well as fish oil supplements, flaxseeds, walnuts, canola, soybeans, and their oils. Generally, a dose of 2 grams per day is recommended.

ACTION STEP 8.1: Log Your Daily Food Intake

This action step focuses on taking an inventory of your eating patterns and building strategies for maintaining a healthy body. First, you'll track your food intake with a food log, which you'll maintain for a week or two using blank pages in your binder. If you have issues with your weight, such as overeating or eating disorders, you may want to use a journal specifically for this purpose so you can track your food and drink intake over a longer period. Your food journal may help your mental health provider diagnose any eating disorders you have and may also help you track the amount you're eating if you start losing a significant amount of weight. You may also want to track any changes in your weight. If you're okay with your weight and simply want to eat healthier, a food log in your binder will be sufficient.

Keeping a food log may help you understand the relationship between your diet and your mood. Using a page in your binder for each day of one month, divide the pages into three columns. In the left column, which you'll label "Time," record the time you ate. In the second column, titled "Food," list what and how much you ate at that time. In the third column, called "Mood," record how you felt at that mealtime. Also record how your mood changed after you ate; for example, you may have initially felt anxious, eaten a muffin, and then felt relaxed. Record any mood changes in the mood column of the log. Here's an example for one day.

Time	Food	Mood
7:30 a.m.	A cup of coffee and a pastry	Upbeat
Noon	Chicken sub and soda	Getting tired
3:00 p.m.	Doughnut and coffee	Sleepy
7:00 p.m.	Burrito and soda	Cranky and sleepy
10:00 p.m.	Cookies and milk	Bored

Keeping a food log will help you understand your relationship with food. Some people use food for comfort and eat more when depressed. Others eat when manic but not when depressed. You may ingest a lot of caffeine without knowing it until you write it down and are confronted with the fact that with chocolate, coffee, and tea, you take in a lot of this mood-altering substance every day. For example, with severe anxiety and the fear that he was heading into a manic episode, James called the on-call nurse at his HMO to get help. After talking for several minutes with the nurse and answering several questions about his coffee intake, James realized that he had drunk six 12-ounce cups of coffee that day. What James experienced was a caffeine-induced anxiety episode, not anxiety related to a manic episode.

Keep your food log for at least one month. Then look for patterns in mood that relate to what you've been eating. For example, do you eat late at night when you're bored or tired? Do you need coffee to get energy in the morning? Are you eating a diet high in unhealthy fats and loaded with sugar? Consult with your health care provider or the nutritionist available for free through the U.S. Department of Agriculture's Food and Nutrition Information

Center website (see the "Resources" section at the end of this chapter) and make a plan for change that will not only improve your mood but also your health.

ACTION STEP 8.2: What and Why Do You Eat?

The goal of this action step is to use the information in your food log to make healthy changes that will improve your health and mood. Again, before making any of these changes, bring your log with you to your health care provider and discuss them. First, answer the following questions:

What are you eating? You may want to consult a nutritionist at the USDA website, or a dietitian or other health care provider to help you with this phase if you find that your eating habits have made you overweight or underweight, or you have illnesses such as hypertension, high cholesterol, heart disease, diabetes, or other diet-related conditions. Any of the latter conditions should motivate you even more to take control of what you put into your mouth. Use the nutrition guidelines provided by the U.S. Department of Agriculture's Food and Nutrition Information Center.

How much coffee, alcohol, green or black tea, or caffeinated sodas do you drink during the week? If you take in more than an average of 250 mg of caffeine per day, you may want to reduce your intake (see the chart in Action Step 8.5 to calculate your daily caffeine consumption). Also limit your intake of sugar-containing drinks, and drink water instead. If you'd like, you can drink flavored water.

When do you drink alcohol and caffeine? At what time of day do you drink alcohol, coffee, and other caffeinated beverages? Avoid drinking caffeinated beverages after noon, because the caffeine may interfere with your sleep. Even modest amounts of caffeine can interfere with sleep. It's important to note that, even when caffeine doesn't interfere with the ability to fall asleep, it can reduce the amount of time spent in deep sleep, thus compromising the quality of sleep. Drinking alcohol in the evening can have the same effect and may interact with some of your medications.

What do you snack on? Are your snacks healthy choices, such as fruit, vegetables, or unbuttered popcorn? If not, try heading to the grocery store with a list of your favorite fruits, vegetables, and other healthy choices. When you return from the store, toss out *most* (all might be too hard to do at once) of the unhealthy choices that are in your cupboards. One trick is to keep fruit in the office refrigerator or your desk drawer to have on hand when you feel the urge to snack at work.

Why are you eating? In your food log, record the feelings you experienced before and after your meals or snacks. Do you notice a pattern of eating when you're tired, bored, or stressed? Remember to observe how you feel after drinking coffee or alcohol. If you find that you're using food or beverages to deal with stress or suppress difficult emotions, you may want to explore alternative strategies for dealing with such issues. Review chapter 5 for ways to cope with stress. Also discuss this with your mental health care provider, so he or she can help you manage your eating habits and promote your mental health and emotional well-being.

ACTION STEP 8.3: Create Your Meal Plan

In this action step, you'll create a meal plan for each week to guide your eating, based on the USDA guidelines found at the Dietary Guidelines for Americans website hosted by the U.S. Department of Health and Human Services (www.health.gov/dietaryguidelines). Basically, the guidelines emphasize fruits, vegetables, whole grains, and fat-free or low-fat milk and milk products. The diet includes lean meats, poultry, fish, beans, eggs, and nuts and is low in saturated fats, trans fats, cholesterol, salt (sodium), and added sugars.

Take a page in your binder and divide it into eight columns, the first for meals and the rest for each day of the week, as shown in the following example.

Use the chart to develop a meal plan for each week, giving yourself room to satisfy your sweet tooth and keep some of your favorite foods while providing enough variety to keep your meals interesting and healthy.

Once you've made your weekly meal plan, use it to make your grocery list. The Dietary Guidelines for Americans website also includes recipes for cooking your healthy choices in a healthy way.

SAMPLE CHART 8.3: Weekly Meal Plan

Food & Drink	Mon	Tues	Wed	Thur	Fri	Sat	Sun
	12/5	12/6	12/7	12/8	12/9	12/10	12/11
Breakfast	Oatmeal, banana	Yogurt	Scrambled eggs	Oatmeal, banana	Cereal, milk	Yogurt	Muffin, coffee
Snack	Orange	Smoothie	Popcorn	Orange	Apple	Nuts	Cheese
Lunch	Sandwich	Veggie soup	Pasta, veggies	Pizza	Salad	Tacos	Brunch buffet
Snack	Carrots	Apple	Grapes	Cookies	Yogurt	Cereal bar	Pastry
Dinner	Grilled chicken, salad	Veggie stir-fry, shrimp	Cheeseburger, fries	Chicken salad	Omelet, salmon	Sushi	Steak

CHART 8.3: Weekly Meal Plan

Food & Drink	Mon	Tues	Wed	Thur	Fri	Sat	Sun
Breakfast							
Snack							
Lunch							
Snack							
Dinner							

CAFFEINE AND ALCOHOL

Alcohol is a mood-altering substance that some people with bipolar disorder use to self-medicate, which means that they use it to either drown their emotions or calm mania. When it comes to alcohol consumption, a good rule to follow is to have none at all because of its possible interaction with many medications. However, if you choose to drink, a safe guideline is to limit yourself to one drink per day, which is equal to one glass of wine, one ounce of spirits, or one 12-ounce can or bottle of beer. Don't drink alcohol within an hour of taking your medications, to avoid possible interactions.

Because caffeine is in so many products and can have such an impact on your mood and sleep patterns, the following question-naire will help you assess your daily intake. The recommended daily intake of caffeine is 250 mg (12 ounces of coffee) or less, to avoid interference with sleep (Barone and Roberts 1996). As you learned in chapter 6, keeping a healthy sleep pattern is an important way to manage bipolar episodes. So, your caffeine intake is very important to your overall mental health. If you find that your caffeine intake is above 250 mg, you'll want to cut back. Also restrict your caffeine intake to the early part of the day so your body will have time to process it before your bedtime.

ACTION STEP 8.4: Assess Your Alcohol Intake

Because alcohol abuse is often a co-occurring disorder, answering the following questions helps you assess your risk of alcohol abuse. The CAGE questionnaire (Ewing 1984) has been widely used and validated for assessing alcohol abuse. The questionnaire is named after the four questions it asks. *If you answer yes to any two questions, seek further help in getting control of your alcohol abuse from your health care provider, or an alcohol or substance abuse counselor or program.*

CAGE Questionnaire

C: Have you ever felt you needed to *cut* down on your drinking?

A: Have people *annoyed* you by criticizing you about your drinking?

G: Have you ever felt *guilty* about your drinking?

E: Have you ever felt you needed a drink first thing in the morning (an *eye-opener*) to steady your nerves or get rid of a hangover?

ACTION STEP 8.5: Assess Your Caffeine Intake

Use this chart to assess your overall caffeine intake during a typical week, not a week when you're traveling or particularly stressed. Make eight copies of the chart. Keep track of your daily caffeine intake for one week using one chart for each day. At the end of the week, average your intake by adding up the totals for each section over the week and dividing by seven to get your average daily intake.

CHART 8.5: Caffeine Consumption

	Amount of caffeine	Ounces, doses, or tablets per day	Total mg per day*
Beverages			
Coffee (6 oz)	125 mg	× _____	= _____
Decaf coffee (6 oz)	5 mg	× _____	= _____
Espresso (1 oz)	50 mg	× _____	= _____
Tea (6 oz)	50 mg	× _____	= _____
Green tea (6 oz)	20 mg	× _____	= _____
Hot cocoa (6 oz)	15 mg	× _____	= _____
Caffeinated soft drinks (12 oz)	40–60 mg	× _____	= _____
Chocolate candy bar	20 mg	× _____	= _____

Over-the-counter medications						
Anacin	32 mg	×	_____	=	_____
Appetite-control pills	100–200 mg	×	_____	=	_____
Dristan	16 mg	×	_____	=	_____
Excedrin	65 mg	×	_____	=	_____
Extra Strength Excedrin	100 mg	×	_____	=	_____
Midol	132 mg	×	_____	=	_____
NoDoz	100 mg	×	_____	=	_____
Triaminicin	30 mg	×	_____	=	_____
Vanquish	33 mg	×	_____	=	_____
Vivarin	200 mg	×	_____	=	_____
Prescription medications						
Cafergot	100 mg	×	_____	=	_____
Fiorinal	40 mg	×	_____	=	_____
Darvon compound	32 mg	×	_____	=	_____
Total mg caffeine per day					_____

HEALTHY EATING AND DRINKING TIPS

Eating nutritious foods and drinking plenty of fluids is an essential component of maintaining both physical and mental health. Based on the latest science at this time, the following paragraphs provide guidance on getting vital nutrition for good health.

Healthy Snacking

Healthy eating doesn't mean giving up snacks. For those of us with bipolar disorder, there are many items we can eat as a snack that are actually good for us and can add to our nutritional daily requirements. My favorites for the office are crunchy apples (they last long without refrigeration and are crunchy or sweet with just a touch of sour). The whole citrus family is also an excellent choice, because they pack enough vitamin C to keep our immune systems going when depression may have lowered our bodies' defenses. Munching on grapes or sunflower seeds is much healthier than eating candy. Grapes keep your mouth busy even though they're mostly water with just enough sugar to keep your taste buds happy. Their high water content may also reduce dry mouth. Sunflower seeds provide you with healthy fats. Another thing to do is keep a bottle of water handy. Drinking lots of water keeps the appetite low, helps kidney and liver functions, and reduces the impact of certain medication side effects.

Surviving Restaurants and Sticking to Your Nutrition Plan

In a restaurant, a trick for keeping your healthy eating patterns is to drink a glass of water before a meal to cleanse your palate and reduce your appetite while keeping you hydrated and minimizing dry mouth. You can ask for half the meal in a take-out box prior to being served so that you can have a smaller portion at the time and another meal later. Ask for salad dressings and sauces on the side so you can control their amounts. Noncreamy salad dressings, such as vinaigrettes, usually contain less unhealthy fat than creamy dressings. And remember, eating a pastry or some ice cream for dessert once or twice a week won't make a huge difference in your life, and you'll more likely stick to your plan if you allow yourself some room to indulge.

Reducing Caffeine and Alcohol Consumption

To reduce your caffeine intake (and keep more money in your wallet), try limiting yourself to one caffeinated drink per day, no more than two cups in volume. Eliminating caffeinated sodas limits your sugar intake as well as your caffeine intake. Because highly refined sugars are harder on your endocrine system than less refined ones, sweeten your coffee with raw sugar instead of white sugar, if available. Take your caffeinated drink no later than noon so it won't interfere with your sleep later. If it's the warmth or taste of a cup of java in the morning that keeps you drinking coffee, try substituting one of your cups of caffeinated coffee with a decaffeinated cup. If you simply need a warm drink in your hand, try drinking hot apple cider or caffeine-free herbal teas. If a buzz is what you seek, try exercising in the morning to give yourself a burst of energy for the day and raise your metabolism so you can burn calories faster.

As mentioned in chapter 6, alcohol can interfere with your sleep and your mood. Minimizing your alcohol intake will reduce its impact on your mood and sleep. If you're having trouble with the amount of alcohol you drink, talk to your mental health provider to see if you have an addiction problem, which is not uncommon among people living with bipolar disorder. Some people use alcohol to calm their mania, or self-medicate, which is never a good idea and should be discussed with your mental health provider. Too much alcohol also interferes with bipolar medication, because many medications interact negatively with alcohol. Having one or two drinks early in the evening, at least an hour before taking your medications, should minimize the impact of alcohol on the effectiveness on your medications and probably won't interfere with your sleep.

What we eat and drink affects our moods directly and indirectly. Caffeine, nicotine (cigarettes), and alcohol are mood-altering substances that should be used in moderation if at all and avoided in the latter part of the day. Don't take anything with caffeine after noon and don't drink alcohol after 8:00 P.M. to limit their effects on your sleep and mood. For those of us with bipolar disorder, keeping track of our food intake can help us identify unhealthy patterns and change our behaviors to promote better health. Making a food plan helps us eat with intention and make good choices for our overall well-being. A diet high in omega-3 fatty acids—available in flaxseeds, walnuts, and salmon (as well as in nutritional supplements)—has been shown to improve mood. A healthy diet focuses on including more whole foods, such as lots of colorful fruits and vegetables, complex carbohydrates, a moderate amount of lean protein, and limiting saturated and trans fats and processed and refined foods. Eating this way will keep your organs, especially your brain, functioning at maximum efficiency.

Here's one way of expanding your diet in a healthy way: On your next trip to the grocery store, try a vegetable or fruit that you've never tried before. Then learn about its nutritional value at the USDA Food and Nutrition Information Center (see the "Resources" section for this chapter) and research recipes on the Internet or in your favorite cookbook. Do this every week until you have incorporated a wide variety of fruits and vegetables into your diet. Try adding one source of omega-3 fatty acids to your meal plan every week until you have a diet rich in these mood-stabilizing nutrients.

RESOURCES

Food and Nutrition Information Center
National Agricultural Library
10301 Baltimore Avenue, Room 105
Beltsville, Maryland 20705
Phone: (301) 504-5414
Fax: (301) 504-6409
E-mail: fnic@nal.usda.gov
Website: http://fnic.nal.usda.gov

You can access a nutritional specialist at the address above. Dietary assessment tools, dietary guideline publications, and resources for monitoring your food intake are copublished by the U.S. Department of Health and Human Services and the U.S. Department of Agriculture, and are available online at www .health.gov/dietaryguidelines.

CHAPTER 9

Build a Support System

A support system is a network of friends, family, and professionals who are willing and able to provide you with the help you need when you need it. This support could vary from accompanying you on medical visits to supporting you in your maintenance plan to sharing in your exercise program. Your friends or family may also be called upon to care for your children, notify your employer in the event of your hospitalization, or implement any emergency plans you've made. Your doctor, therapist, nurse, or other medical provider is also an important part of your support network, and having a professional to call in a crisis can really make a difference. It's important to realize that you won't get support if no one knows you need it, and support is vital to your recovery and maintenance plan. In fact, having a support system may save your life. A review of past studies found that, along with medication adherence and psychotherapy, social support is a significant factor in extending survival times of people living with bipolar disorder (Altman et al. 2006).

TYPES OF SUPPORT

You may need several types of support to maintain a healthy lifestyle, reduce your triggers, and minimize your symptoms. Here are some of the types of support you might want to investigate:

- Emotional support is best described as a shoulder to lean on when you don't feel very strong. A good listener who's unlikely to judge is the best person from whom to seek emotional support. Good emotional support is having someone to call in the middle of the night when you're afraid or anxious, or simply can't sleep. You can seek emotional support from a family member or friend, the on-call nurse of your HMO, or a hotline.

- Getting support in healthy living and following your maintenance plan is a general kind of support you can get from friends, family, and professionals. Many people in your life can play significant roles in supporting your quest for a healthy lifestyle. You can have exercise buddies or a trainer who keeps you accountable. Someone with whom you live might be a good support for you in taking your medications. An online network or group can also provide support in living a healthy lifestyle, including encouraging you to take your medications and attend psychotherapy sessions.

- Help with your responsibilities, such as taking care of your home, children, and pets, is the kind of support you might ask of someone with whom you live, or family or close friends who live nearby. Perhaps you have a nanny, housekeeper, or pet-sitter who can be ready to take over when you're unable to carry out your daily responsibilities.

- Treatment support is the encouragement to follow your treatment plan as outlined by your mental health care provider. Support groups of any kind are great for helping you stick to your treatment plan. Your psychotherapist and other medical providers are also good sources of support for maintaining your treatment plan.

- Financial support may be necessary if you aren't working or are recovering from over-shopping during a manic episode. It's often difficult to find someone who'll provide you with emergency funds when you need them, but family and close friends are usually the best source of such support.

■ Getting support from your employer is useful in maintaining your employment, but because of the risk of stigma or the potential consequences of telling people at work, many people try to find support for work-related issues through other support networks. However, if your employer is supportive, your work situation can be adapted to help you maintain wellness and reduce work-related stress.

■ Crisis support is necessary when things aren't going well. In a crisis situation, you may require many different forms of support on very short notice at any time of day or night. The person from whom to seek crisis support is someone who is dependable and has previously agreed to provide this kind of support. You may also call an on-call nurse or crisis hotline.

■ Support groups, whether online or in person, are a great place to find people who know what you're going through and can give you the kind of support you need. To find the right support group for you, check to see if you agree with the group's philosophy. Time and location of group meetings are also important, and online groups allow you the flexibility of getting support when you need it from a large group of people around the country. A support group is right for you if you feel comfortable sharing with the group and supported by the people in the group. You may find the right group for you on the first try, or you may have to visit more than one group until you find a support group "home." One example of an online support group is dailystrength.org.

BUILDING A SUPPORT NETWORK

You may already have a support network without being aware of it, or you may have to consciously seek out trustworthy people to whom you disclose your bipolar disorder and let them know how they can help you stay well. It's important to be deliberate in your efforts to build a support network that can sufficiently promote your mental wellness and be there for you in an emergency.

Telling Others About Your Bipolar Disorder

Telling people about your bipolar disorder can be one of the most challenging tasks in building a support network that works for you. You may risk rejection, disappointment, and stigmatization when you tell others, so be prepared for this even though you'll only tell people who care about you and are close to you. Many people have stereotypical ideas about the mentally ill and may be unable to reconcile their image of you with their image of a mentally ill person. However, the benefits of letting go of the secrecy of your illness are worth the risk of having some people misunderstand. This is an opportunity for you to educate others about your illness, which may actually help reduce stigmatization and discrimination in the long run.

The people who will become members of your support network are those who are most understanding when you share your story or who offer assistance in response. Giving your loved ones a brochure that explains mental illness generally, and bipolar disorder specifically, is a very helpful gesture that can provide them with answers to questions they may have later. In healthy relationships, we communicate openly and acknowledge our feelings, but all relationships go through difficult periods. Telling others may cause tensions in your relationships, but being open about who you are, and willing to hear and understand how others feel, will ultimately strengthen your relationships.

Some people may have a hard time understanding at first but simply need time and more information to come around. The people who should know are those closest to you, who are likely to have experienced, or experience in the future, the impact of your illness. It's only fair to your loved ones to let them understand why you behaved in ways you did in the past. Some may be slow to warm up to the idea, but now you'll know who your friends really are. Telling no one is *not* an option! Secrecy fosters the isolation that sabotages symptom management. Everyone needs a support system, because as the saying goes (to paraphrase John Donne's original writing), "No one is an island."

TIPS FOR TELLING OTHERS

Telling other people about your bipolar disorder isn't easy, so here are some tips to help you take the first step to getting the support you need. Specific instructions for telling different groups of people appear a little later, but this is a starting point. It's not necessary to tell everyone in your life about your bipolar disorder. For example, people with whom you have little contact or an insignificant relationship don't need to know. Nor do you want to start by telling people who may be unsupportive.

Start with the people closest to you whose lives may have been affected by your illness. They'll appreciate knowing the reason for your past behavior. Also consider telling people who have helped you in the past when you experienced symptoms but who didn't necessarily know you had bipolar disorder. They're most likely to be helpful in the future, and they deserve an explanation for your behavior. Lower down on the list are people who probably won't be supportive or understanding. Having some success at telling people who are supportive will give you the strength to tell those who may be less supportive. Action Step 9.1 will ask you to make a list of the people you'd like to talk to about your bipolar disorder, in order of level of supportiveness. Once you've decided whom to tell, here are some tips on how to approach the conversation.

1. Find a time and place to talk when and where you're calm and free of distractions. Public places are poor choices. Instead invite the person to your home and keep the television and radio off. If it's your employer, ask for an uninterrupted period and meet in a private office with the door closed. Choose a quiet, private location where you can talk for at least an hour, and be ready to answer questions about your illness and what it means for those around you. One way to start the conversation is to say, "I'd like to tell you something that's important to me. Afterward, feel free to ask any questions you may have. I have a serious illness and am working on getting and staying healthy. It's bipolar disorder. Do you know what that is? It's a

chronic but treatable condition that results in mood swings between depression and mania."

2. When talking to the other person about your bipolar disorder, stick to simple facts about the illness and briefly describe how it affects you. Depending on the relationship you have with this person, you may choose to start by saying how much you care about him or her and how much he or she means to you, and that this is why you've chosen to speak with him or her about your illness. If you've caused the person any pain during one of your episodes, you may want to add an apology and explain that your behavior was a result of your illness.

3. Give the other person the opportunity to ask questions, as well as a list of resources, such as books and websites. You can answer the person's questions, then refer him or her to this book, brochures you may have chosen for such occasions, or websites such as those of the National Institute of Mental Health (www.nimh.nih.gov), the National Alliance on Mental Illness (www.nami.org), or the Depression and Bipolar Support Alliance (www.dbsalliance.org). (You can also get helpful brochures at these websites.)

4. If you know of something in particular that this person could do to support your wellness program, you may choose to mention it after all his or her questions have been answered, your conversation has become more comfortable, and the person shows supportiveness.

Next, we'll discuss how to tell your loved ones about your illness, the types of support to ask for, and how to ask for what you need.

Telling Your Adult Family Members

You may choose to tell your family individually or as a group. You could break the news at a family gathering or start with parents or siblings. Factors to consider are how close your relationship is to each family member, how open you think they'll be to hearing what you have to say, and how supportive they're likely to be. Consider family therapy for your immediate family, including your children. This may help your family explore their feelings, and understand how your illness affects you and how they can be a part of your treatment plan.

Telling Your Children

Telling your children is a very difficult task, one that will vary according to the ages of your children. The older your child, the more details you can provide about your symptoms and treatment. A young child may simply need to know that you're sick but taking steps to feel better. You may say something like "Mommy (or Daddy) isn't feeling well but is going to the doctor to feel better." If you have had depression or manic symptoms, your children have probably noticed the changes in you, so giving them a context in which to understand your behavior will help relieve some of their fear and confusion about your behavior. Be careful to avoid making your children feel responsible for your symptoms. Reassure your children that you're getting treatment and will make sure that they'll always be taken care of. Encourage your children to share their feelings and questions. Apologize for any pain you may have caused them during an episode and assure them that you're working hard to avoid having it happen again.

Telling Your Friends

Telling friends may be more difficult than telling family members, depending on the length and nature of the friendship. Some of your friends may have already experienced your mania or depression, which may help you explain to them what bipolar disorder is and how it affects your life. The conditions for telling friends are similar to those for telling family. If you have a group of friends with whom you spend a lot of time, you might have them over for dinner and tell them all at once. If you have individual friends who don't know each other, you'll need to tell them one at a time. Taking a walk or meeting in a park or a private location is a good setting for this important conversation.

Telling Your Romantic Partner

Telling your romantic partner is a particular challenge potentially made easier by realizing that he or she has probably noticed symptoms of your illness and that sharing this information may help explain your behavior. As part of this disclosure, you may also want to discuss the sexual implications of some of your medications, or your depressive or manic episodes. If you have a strong relationship with your partner, this discussion can bring you closer. Make a special time to have this conversation, avoiding dinnertime and bedtime. If you have alienated your partner as a result of the behaviors associated with your illness, you may choose to tell him or her in front of a third party, such as a psychotherapist or religious leader, who can help you discuss any related issues.

If you're dating someone new, tell him or her as soon as you feel comfortable enough to do so. This is important information that your partner will need to know if you want to have an open, honest relationship with him or her. This also helps your partner provide the support you need. It's much better for you to spend your energy on getting better than on protecting your secret.

If you're single and on the dating scene, you may want to know when is the right time to tell your new love interest. The first date is much too early. Whenever the relationship is becoming serious is the right time to share this information about yourself. It's an important part of who you are, and anyone who's getting close to you should have this information to know you better and understand what issues he or she may have to deal with, presently or in the future. It's only fair to allow the other person to assess his or her relationship with you. Although your treatment and maintenance plan may be keeping you stable, you may have mood fluctuations that affect the relationship. Most likely you'll need support from your partner if you experience symptoms, because he or she will be close enough to you to see changes in your behavior. Asking your partner to inform you of any changes he or she sees in your behavior and giving your partner access to others in your support network are good ways to include him or her in your support network.

Telling Your Coworkers or Employer

Consider carefully whether to tell your coworkers or employer because of the potential implications on your job and the possibility of stigmatization in the workplace. If you've had job performance issues in the past, telling your employer may help him or her understand why you had these problems. Also take the opportunity to let your employer know that you're actively seeking treatment, which will improve your future performance. It may be helpful to consult with your human resources department before talking with your immediate superiors. Remember that you have certain rights under the Americans with Disabilities Act; you may choose to ask for reasonable accommodations that would allow you to improve your performance. It's a good idea to consult with a lawyer before talking to anyone at your workplace so you can understand the legal and financial implications of your decision.

THE ANXIETY OF DISCLOSING YOUR BIPOLAR DISORDER

It's natural to feel anxious when telling someone you care about that you have a chronic and severe illness. Try some of the relaxation techniques you learned in chapter 5 to deal with this stressful situation. Doing deep breathing exercises and writing down what you want to say will help increase your confidence in facing this challenge.

To deal with the risk of rejection and stigmatization, talk to your mental health care provider about strategies that might work for you. You can also consult online resources, such as the National Alliance on Mental Illness (www.nami.org) and the Depression and Bipolar Support Alliance (www.dbsalliance.org). If you experience rejection or negative emotions when telling someone, here are a few ways to respond:

- "I understand that this is a difficult thing to hear so I'll give you the time you need to get used to the idea."

■ "I'm sorry you feel this way. If you ever want to talk more about it, I'm willing to have this conversation again and answer any questions you have."

■ "I wasn't expecting this response from you, and although my feelings are hurt, I know that this is a difficult thing to hear about someone you love. If you have fears about this, I can give you some resources that may answer your questions."

Rejection hurts, especially when the pain is caused by someone close to you. Depending on whom you plan to tell, you may want to get help in telling others. For example, after talking with your partner, you may ask him or her to join you in speaking with family and mutual friends. Doing this as a team may provide you with the emotional support you need.

ACTION STEP 9.1: Whom Do You Want to Tell?

In your binder, list the people you plan to tell about your bipolar disorder in order of importance, with the most important person first. In making this list, consider how supportive each person will be, how close your relationship is, and his or her existing relationship with your bipolar disorder. For example, if the person has dealt directly with your manic or depressive symptoms, then explaining your behavior will be helpful to him or her and to your relationship.

YOUR PROVIDER'S ROLE IN YOUR SUPPORT NETWORK

Your medical and mental health providers are an important part of your support network. They can work with you to develop your treatment plan, and you can use them as a resource in helping you build your support system. If you're in counseling, you can use your sessions to develop strategies for disclosing your mental illness. You can practice what you plan to say during your sessions and possibly even invite loved ones, such as your partner or children, to a session so you can disclose your disorder with your therapist's support. This would allow your loved ones an opportunity to ask your provider questions about the disorder and learn how to become an integral part of your support system.

Your health care provider can also help you decide if you need a medical advance directive in case you need to be hospitalized against your will. A medical advance directive is a living will or durable power of attorney for health care. In this document you give directions about future medical care you're likely to receive. In this case, your medical advance directive would include directions for the type of medical care you want to receive specific to your bipolar disorder. You can consult your health care provider to discuss who should have the privilege of accessing your health care information in case you experience debilitating symptoms and need hospitalization. Typically, the people with this type of access are parents, spouses or domestic partners, or close and trustworthy friends.

Including your support network in your treatment plan is something to discuss with your health care provider. He or she can help you determine who'd be the best person to accompany you to therapy visits, medical appointments, or support groups and whom to ask for various types of support.

ADDING PEOPLE TO YOUR SUPPORT NETWORK

If you don't have much of a support network, you'll need to connect with people who can support you in staying well. In other words, it's time for you to start making friends.

Support Groups

Some of the best places to start adding to your support system are bipolar or mental illness support groups. Members of support groups often understand your bipolar experience better than those who don't have the disorder, and will get to know you over time as you attend the sessions. If you've never attended a support group, now's the time to start. You may need to visit more than one support group before finding one where you feel comfortable. You can find lists of local support groups from the NAMI and DBSA websites or their local offices, or from your health care provider. The keys to evaluating a support group are feeling safe talking about your emotions and thoughts, and sensing that you share something in common with the other group members. If the group has a facilitator, check his or her qualifications and experience for running such a group. Look for a degree in social work, counseling, psychology, nursing, or medicine and experience in running groups. For self-run groups, you should feel comfortable with the process of the group and the way its leadership is structured.

Other Types of Groups

If you attend a group exercise program, perhaps a yoga or spinning class, you can develop a friendly relationship with someone who shares your commitment to staying healthy through exercise. If you're only friendly before, during, or after exercise, you may want to extend an invitation for coffee or a smoothie after your exercise class and see how your friendship grows from there. Religious institutions are also good places to find people with whom to develop friendships. Most religious institutions offer opportunities for social networking through various groups or volunteer opportunities.

If you're taking a class and are part of a study group with whom you spend a lot of time, you can include the group as part of your social support network or choose one or two individuals with whom you feel some connection. To begin a friendship, you can start by saying hello to someone you've casually conversed with before, during, or after the class. You can talk about something that happened in class and then extend an invitation for coffee, a movie, dinner, or shopping to find class-related gear or equipment. You may not make a connection on your first attempt, but if you have few friends now, the effort it takes to persist is worth the eventual payoff in social support.

You may also have colleagues at work with whom you've developed a good working relationship. Perhaps you could invite them to a social event, such as bowling or a movie, outside of working hours. Getting involved in volunteer activities can bring you in touch with others who share your interests, and helping others is also a way to prevent or alleviate the symptoms of depression. Joining groups focused on specific interests or activities, such as book clubs, knitting groups, or chess clubs, is a good way to find people with whom you have things in common and therefore can develop supportive friendships.

Asking for Support

Seek emotional support from people who've already shown that they're there for you. This isn't a job for new friends unless they've shown the willingness to lend an ear when you needed one. Household help can be left to people you live with or a friend. You can also hire a professional cleaning service to take care of your house when you're unable to do so. Child care or pet care can also be left to professionals or to friends who've already developed a relationship with your children or pets. An emergency is not the time for children to have to get to know unfamiliar people.

Determining what you need and who can help you is a task best done in collaboration with your health care provider. First, make a list of the types of support you may need, including anything from child care to exercise program support to accompaniment for your blood draws to help running errands to encouragement to get out of bed when you're depressed.

Tips for Asking for Help

In a culture that emphasizes taking care of oneself, it can be difficult to admit you need help and harder still to ask for it. Asking for help takes courage but is evidence of your commitment to maintaining your mental health. Your pride is not worth losing your health, and most people accept giving their help as an expected part of friendship. People who really care about you want to see you healthy and will be ready to give you the help you need if you're ready to ask for it. Here are some tips on asking for help:

1. When considering asking someone for help, consider his or her ability to provide the help you need. Is he familiar enough with your town to help drive you to errands if you need that? Is she attentive enough to adequately take care of your pets or plants? Does his schedule permit him to drive you to and from doctor's appointments? Also consider how much help the person has provided in the past. If she has never seemed interested in providing help to you, you can still ask her, but don't be surprised if she declines. If you need help with your children, select someone who already has a good relationship with them as well as the time and energy to take care of them. You can choose someone else to accompany you on medical visits, help you manage your household, or simply lend an ear.

2. Start your sentences with "I need ..." or "I feel ..." Follow up with "It would be helpful if you could ..." or "This will help me ..."

3. Be specific about what you need. For example, if you need help with your children, tell the person when and for how long you need help.

4. Give the person the opportunity to ask questions that will help him or her get a clear understanding of what you need and how best he or she can help.

5. If someone is willing to help, thank him or her for the offer, and if the person can't help you in the way you need, thank him or her for considering it. Don't conclude that someone's inability to help is a reflection of your friendship. Instead it may simply be that the person can't help at that time. Use your emotional support network, including your health care providers, to help you deal with any negative feelings you have if, and when, your requests for assistance are rejected.

6. When you get the help you need, remember to thank those who helped you. Be careful to avoid using only one person for social support, because he or she could get tired. Look for multiple sources of support. You'll also get the benefit of different perspectives.

7. Also use local hotlines and support groups, online support groups, and your health care provider's on-call staff, if they have one.

CRISIS SUPPORT

You may follow all the advice given in this book, take your medications as prescribed, and regularly visit your therapist but still find yourself having a manic or depressive episode. It helps to make plans in advance for the times when you find it hard to take care of yourself. Planning for a mental health crisis helps you get the treatment you need quickly and effectively. Including your support people in your crisis plan will allow them to act on your behalf if you're having symptoms but are in denial about needing help. Also, they can access help when you're unable to ask for it yourself.

Your crisis plan may include preparing the following:

- A list of your support network, including their roles in your life and their contact information.

- A list of all medications you're taking and why you're taking them, and a list of your health care providers and pharmacy.

- A list of symptoms that may indicate the need to have others take over your care.

- A list of instructions for your support network should you become unable to take care of yourself. Include information for practical things such as paying your bills and making financial decisions. Your partner, if you have one, may be best suited for this role, because you might have joint accounts that make it easy for him or her to support you in this area.

- A list of people who are available to drive you to appointments or the hospital if required.

- Directions for care of your children and pets in case you become unable to take care of them yourself.

- Directions for notifying your employer and loved ones in the case of your hospitalization.

- Your insurance information.

- An advance medical directive and a legal power of attorney, if you choose, created in consultation with your doctor and legal counsel, for implementation if you become unable to care for yourself.

It's best to keep this information in a folder in a central location known to more than one member of your support system, and also have your health care provider keep a copy. Consider also providing copies to one or two people with whom you have a close relationship and can trust to implement your requests. Lastly, in your wallet it's wise to keep emergency contact information that includes your health insurance number, the contact information of at least three people to be notified in case of emergency, and the contact information for your health care providers.

ACTION STEP 9.2: Whom to Ask for Support

Here are some types of support you may need. On a sheet of paper from your binder, list one to three people who could provide you with each type of support. Also include their contact information, such as e-mail, addresses, and telephone numbers.

- ■ Emotional support

- ■ Financial support

- ■ Care for children or pets

- ■ Household help

- ■ Accompaniment to appointments

- ■ Crisis support

Asking for support is difficult, but once you've determined the best sources for each type of assistance, thinking of ways to ask for help will be much easier. Asking for help entails a willingness to suffer potential rejection and disappointment, but the more carefully you've thought through your choices, the better your chances of success. And the more time you put in to planning your conversations about either disclosing or seeking help for your bipolar disorder, the more productive those conversations will be. You now have many resources for help in building a solid support system.

CHAPTER 10

Advocate for Yourself

Advocating for yourself means speaking up to get what you need. This chapter focuses on advocating for good medical and psychological treatment for your bipolar disorder when you feel you're not getting what you need to keep your symptoms at bay and promote your mental health.

PATIENT'S RIGHTS

Many health care providers have policies that include a set of patient's rights that all health care providers under their jurisdiction are expected to respect. If you have Medicaid or Medicare coverage, you're also protected by a patient's bill of rights. Most of these bills of rights give patients the following rights:

- Access to information

- Privacy

- Being treated with respect and dignity without prejudice or discrimination

- Choosing a health care provider

- Giving or withholding consent to care

The American Psychological Association has adopted a Mental Health Patient's Bill of Rights that outlines the principles for the provision of mental health and substance abuse treatment services. (To get a copy, see the "Resources" section at the end of this chapter.) It covers topics such as professional expertise, choice, appeals and grievances, nondiscrimination, and treatment review.

Get to know the details of your rights and responsibilities related to your own health care provider by reading the patient guide that comes from your insurer; contact your insurer's customer service representative if you have any questions. If you're uninsured, ask your provider for a written document outlining your rights, and where and how you can get your questions answered. You cannot advocate for yourself without having the information you need, so knowing your rights is crucial.

STANDING UP FOR YOURSELF WITH YOUR HEALTH CARE PROVIDER

If you want more information about your illness, treatment, or coverage, ask for clarification. Write down the questions you want answered and use them as your script for getting the information you need. If you're not assertive, ask a friend to go with you to important appointments and support you in asking questions if there's anything you don't understand. Before going to the appointment, consult your provider to be sure that bringing a friend is okay. If your friend can't be with you during the meeting, you may still feel supported if your friend comes with you and waits for you until your appointment is over. Discuss your wishes and concerns with your friend, especially any questions you want to have answered. Ask your friend to help make sure you get the answers you need.

Discussing Medications and Their Effects

Only you know how you feel, so it's your job to tell your provider when you're not feeling okay. It's also your job to tell your health care provider when the side effects of medication interfere with your willingness to follow through on your treatment plan. Ask your health care provider for other medication options, discuss the benefits and drawbacks of each choice, and then make a decision based on this information. Although your medical provider may make suggestions regarding the medication regimen that's best for you, it's up to you to make the final decision. Some HMOs or insurance providers may have restrictions on the type of care or medication that's covered. If the choice you and your doctor think is best isn't covered by your insurer, then being your best advocate means you must contact your insurer and begin an appeal (see your patient manual) so you can get the care or medication that will keep you well.

FINDING ANOTHER PROVIDER

If you feel you're not getting what you want from your health care provider, consider finding another provider using the procedures in Action Step 1.6. This is a big decision that can have a great impact on your care, so make sure that you've tried advocating for yourself and working with your provider. Let your provider know that you're not satisfied with your patient-provider relationship and that you're seeking another provider. If you're comfortable with the idea, you can ask your current provider for a referral. Once you find another provider, request a transfer of your medical records to your new provider and follow up to make sure they are transferred in a timely manner.

MENTAL HEALTH PARITY LAWS

Most U.S. states have mental health parity, which means that people with mental illness have the right to receive the same level of care as those with other illnesses. If your state doesn't have this, consider joining a grassroots advocacy organization such as the Bipolar and Depression Support Alliance (BDSA) or National Alliance on Mental Illness (NAMI). These organizations have support groups for people with bipolar disorder and their loved ones, and also advocate on behalf of people living with mental illnesses. Getting on their mailing lists will keep you informed and allow you to participate in political advocacy by telling your story and writing your elected officials to fight for policies that provide the care and support you need to get and stay well.

FORCED HOSPITALIZATION

With regard to being hospitalized without your permission, each state's laws differ, so this topic can only be discussed briefly. The first step is to get to know the rules in your state. A good source for this information is your local NAMI or BDSA chapter. Let your key social support people know your state's rules for forced hospitalization and also let them know your wishes so they can advocate on your behalf. In many states, you can be hospitalized if a medical provider assesses that you're a danger to yourself or others. It's also a good idea to write a medical directive (you can get a copy from your health care provider) outlining the kind of care you want if you become unable to make important decisions at the time of your hospitalization.

ACTION STEP 10.1: What You Need to Know

Get a file folder or a large envelope and label it "Advocacy." In this file or envelope, keep important documents that you'll need for supporting your advocacy efforts.

- Your medical directive

- A copy of the Americans with Disabilities Act

- A copy of your medical health insurer's patient manual

- A copy of your employer's human resources manual, especially as it relates to sick benefits

- A copy of the American Psychological Association's Mental Health Patient's Bill of Rights (www.apa.org/topics/rights)

- A doctor's letter certifying your exact diagnosis

These documents will give you the information you need to advocate for yourself, because as the saying from Sir Francis Bacon goes, "Knowledge is power."

ADVOCATING FOR YOURSELF WITH CREDITORS

Many people living with bipolar disorder end up with credit problems because of the shopping sprees that can accompany mania and the lack of attention to bills that can come with depression. You may need to explain your situation to your creditors so you can have time to rebuild a good credit rating now that you're working toward becoming more stable. You can start with the billing department and say, "I've been ill, and these charges are a result of my illness. I'd like to repay my debt and wonder if I can have my payments or interest reduced for the next six months until I can get back on my feet." If they can't help you, ask to speak to a supervisor. If the supervisor can't help you, ask if there's someone else you can speak with or write to who may be able to help you with your request.

If you're in a lot of debt and can't see your way out, consider contacting a nonprofit, free, credit counseling service, such as Consumer Credit Counseling Service (which has local branches across the country), to help you make a budget and pay your bills. If you have a shopping problem when depressed or manic, proactive financial decision making may include having only one credit card and leaving it at home when you go out, reserving it only for emergencies. If you feel you're not the best person to take care of your finances, you can have your spouse, partner, or someone else you trust help you write a budget, keep track of your finances, or pay your bills.

ADVOCATING FOR YOURSELF AT WORK

Thursday, December 8, 2005

Today I met with my boss, and she basically told me to go on medical leave for one quarter while I focus on getting better. Seems that things in my classes were worse than I thought.

When I wrote the above journal entry, I felt that I couldn't advocate for myself. My whole world had come crashing down on me, and I was willing to be swept away by the flow—but not for long. My wonderful support system stepped in and helped me advocate for myself. I didn't know my employer's human resources rules applicable to my situation. I knew the Americans with Disabilities Act to the extent it was covered in my social policy class, but I'd never thought of it applying to me. Don't let yourself end up in that situation. Know what you're entitled to at work by getting a copy of your organization's health-related policies. And know this before you need to know it. If you don't yet have a copy of your employer's health benefits policy, make it a point to get one the next time you're at work.

AMERICANS WITH DISABILITIES ACT

Title I of the Americans with Disabilities Act of 1990 (ADA) prohibits private employers, state and local governments, employment agencies, and labor unions from discriminating against qualified individuals with disabilities in job application procedures, hiring, firing, advancement, compensation, and job training, as well as other terms, conditions, and privileges of employment. (Refer to www.eeoc.gov/policy/ada.html.)

The ADA covers employers with fifteen or more employees, including state and local agencies. It also applies to employment agencies and labor organizations. The ADA's nondiscrimination standards also apply to federal sector employees.

According to the ADA, an individual with a disability is a person who meets one of the following conditions:

- Has a physical or mental impairment that substantially limits one or more major life activities

- Has a record of such an impairment

- Is regarded as having such an impairment

The ADA specifies that a qualified employee or applicant with a disability is an individual who, with or without reasonable accommodation, can perform the essential functions of the job in question.

An employer is required to make a reasonable accommodation to the known disability of a qualified applicant or employee if it would not impose an "undue hardship" on the operation of the employer's business. Undue hardship is defined as an action requiring significant difficulty or expense when considered in light of factors such as an employer's size, financial resources, and the nature and structure of its operation.

An employer is not required to lower quality or production standards to make an accommodation; nor is an employer obligated to provide personal-use items, such as glasses or hearing aids.

According to the ADA, job discrimination against people with disabilities is illegal if practiced by private employers, state and local governments, employment agencies, labor organizations, and labor-management committees. If you work for one of these types of employers, you're protected under the ADA and can request accommodations that will keep you healthy and help you be a productive employee. If you feel that your employer is discriminating against you because of your bipolar disorder, first go to your human resources department to file a formal complaint and go through its process. If you aren't satisfied with this process, seek redress through the local office of the U.S. Equal Employment Opportunity Commission (www.eeoc.gov) by submitting an intake questionnaire by mail or in person. The intake questionnaire is available online and through your local office. If there's no office near you, contact the nearest office by phone to receive a form, and then submit it by mail. At any point in this process, ask questions when you don't understand something, and if you think you need further assistance, seek legal counsel.

REASONABLE ACCOMMODATION

The ADA defines reasonable accommodation as any change or adjustment to a job or work environment that permits a qualified applicant or employee with a disability to participate in the job application process, perform the essential functions of a job, or receive benefits and privileges of employment equal to those of employees without disabilities. For example, reasonable accommodation may include the following:

- Job restructuring

- Part-time or modified work schedule

- Reassignment to a vacant position

- Adjusting or modifying examinations, training materials, or policies

- Making the workplace readily accessible to and usable by people with disabilities

After you've been hired, your employer is restricted from asking that you take a medical examination or asking questions about your disability unless they are related to your job and necessary to conduct your employer's business.

MENTAL ILLNESS STIGMA IN THE WORKPLACE

Unless you need accommodations, there's no reason to tell your employer about your mental illness. You never know how the stigma of mental illness might play out in your workplace. To help you decide, consider the history of your company in this area. Have your employer and coworkers reacted compassionately to other employees who've been ill? Are any other employees known to be mentally ill? Has your boss or have your colleagues ever discussed people who are mentally ill? What was the nature of these discussions?

If you choose to disclose your illness, you may find it helpful to write a script so that you don't forget anything important and your nervousness doesn't get in the way of saying what you want to say exactly as you want to say it. Also know what accommodations you're seeking before you start these very important conversations. You might ask for a flexible schedule or the opportunity to work from home to accommodate appointments or medication side effects. You might also discuss work assignments that may trigger your symptoms and see if you can be assigned other tasks. If you're having a particularly difficult time with your symptoms, consider asking for a part-time schedule to reduce the stress of having many commitments.

Depending on the nature of your symptoms, you may decide to refrain from telling your employer, especially if you don't need workplace accommodations. Or, you may choose to disclose in order to come out of the mentally ill "closet." You may already have experienced symptoms on the job and find it best to explain your behavior so that your performance can be placed in context. If you plan to tell your boss, it's a good idea to start with your human resources department, which may help you develop a strategy for breaking the news to your boss. Telling your employer is a big decision to make only after weighing all the pros and cons. Consult with your support group (if you attend one) about their experiences and any tips they may have for you. Lastly, if you can afford it, consider consulting a lawyer to gain clarity about your rights and develop a strategy for disclosing this important information to your employer.

GOVERNMENT ASSISTANCE FOR DISABLED WORKERS

Maybe you're unable to work because of your bipolar disorder and want to apply for disability benefits. The U.S. Social Security Administration provides two benefits for the mentally ill: Supplemental Security Income (SSI) for people who are poor, disabled, and unable to work, and Social Security Disability Insurance (SSDI) for people who are poor, disabled, and unable to work but have worked in the past or whose parents worked and contributed into the system.

Eligibility for SSI or SSDI

Eligibility for either SSI or SSDI through the Social Security Administration (SSA) is challenging because the standard of disability is high. However, if your symptoms are severe enough to interfere with your ability to work, you may qualify for one of the two programs. You can get a form at the SSA website at www.ssa .gov or from your local SSA office, which you can find in your phone directory (or online at www.socialsecurity.gov/locator), and get someone at the office help you with your application.

Anyone may apply for SSI, but you must have worked previously to qualify for SSDI. There's no charge for the application process for either SSI or SSDI. As outlined by the SSA, your rights for either program are as follows:

- You have the right to apply.

- You have the right to receive help from Social Security.

- You have the right to a representative.

- You have the right to a notice (about decisions).

- You have the right to appeal.

The SSA uses several criteria to determine disability and bipolar disorder is a qualifying illness, but your experience of bipolar disorder must be debilitating to the point where you cannot work at all. Under the SSI program, there are no benefits payable for short-term or partial disability.

Qualifying as disabled requires a long interview with the SSA staff and the completion of many forms. It's usually a slow and arduous process requiring perseverance, patience, and determination. Advocate for yourself in this process by seeking legal assistance or using the services, because most cases get denied on the first try. But if you're truly disabled, be prepared to fight for the legitimacy of your case to get the benefits to which you're entitled.

Having a mental illness is a challenging experience that affects many spheres of your life. Although your health care provider may have medical training that gives him or her the necessary skills and knowledge to help you, ultimately you're the one who has to live with your illness, so you'll have to advocate for yourself to get the help you want and need to maintain your wellness. Hopefully, you'll have a productive relationship with your health care provider that requires little advocacy on your part, but it's good to be prepared in case this is required of you. Advocating in the workplace can be challenging, but if you have a sympathetic employer, you may be able to get the accommodations that reduce your stress and maximize your productivity. You may need to negotiate in other areas of your life, and the more you have to stand up for yourself, the better you'll get at it.

RESOURCES

Mental Health Patient's Bill of Rights
American Psychological Association
750 First Street NE, Washington, D.C. 20002-4242
Phone: (800) 374-2721
E-mail: order@apa.org
Website: www.apa.org/topics/rights

References

Altman, S., S. Haeri, L. Cohen, A. Ten, E. Barron, I. I. Galynker, and
K. N. Duhamel. 2006. Predictors of relapse in bipolar disorder: A
review. *Journal of Psychiatric Practice* 12 (5):269–82.

American Heart Association. 2008. Fish and omega-3 fatty acids.
Accessed at www.americanheart.org/presenter.jhtml?identifier=
4632 on June 15, 2008.

APA (American Psychiatric Association). 2000. *Diagnostic and
Statistical Manual of Mental Disorders.* 4th ed. (text revision).
Washington, DC: American Psychiatric Publishing, Inc. www
.nimh.nih.gov/health/publications/bipolar-disorder/introduction
.shtml (accessed June 15, 2008).

Americans with Disabilities Act. 1990. *U.S. Code* 42, § 12101, reprinted
by U.S. Equal Employment Opportunity Commission at www
.eeoc.gov/policy/ada.html (accessed March 11, 2008).

Baldassano, C. F., L. B. Marangell, L. Gyulai, S. N. Ghaemi, H. Joffe, D. R. Kim, K. Sagduyu, C. J. Truman, S. R. Wisniewski, G. S. Sachs, and L. S. Cohen. 2005. Gender differences in bipolar disorder: Retrospective data from the first 500 STEP-BD participants. *Bipolar Disorders* 7:465–70.

Bale, G. L. 2006. Stress sensitivity and the development of affective disorders. *Hormones and Behavior* 50 (4):529–33.

Barbour, K. A., T. M. Edenfield, and J. A. Blumenthal. 2007. Exercise as a treatment for depression and other psychiatric disorders: A review. *Journal of Cardiopulmonary Rehabilitation and Prevention* 27 (6):359–67.

Barone, J. J., and H. R. Roberts. 1996. Caffeine consumption. *Food and Chemical Toxicology* 34 (1):119–29.

Bauer, M., P. Grof, N. Rasgon, T. Bschor, T. Glenn, and P. C. Whybrow. 2006. Temporal relation between sleep and mood in patients with bipolar disorder. *Bipolar Disorder* 8 (2):160–67.

Brostedt, E. M., and N. L. Pedersen. 2003. Stressful life events and affective illness. *Acta Psychiatrica Scandinavica* 107 (3):208–15.

Chiu, C. C., S. Y. Huang, C. C. Chen, and K. P. Su. 2005. Omega-3 fatty acids are more beneficial in the depressive phase than in the manic phase in patients with bipolar I disorder. *Journal of Clinical Psychiatry* 66 (6):1613–14.

Choi, B. C., A. W. Pak, J. C. Choi, and E. C. Choi. 2007. Daily step goal of 10,000 steps: A literature review. *Clinical and Investigative Medicine* 30 (3):E146–51.

Cohen, A., C. Hammen, R. M. Henry, and S. E. Daley. 2004. Effects of stress and social support on recurrence in bipolar disorder. *Journal of Affective Disorders* 82 (1):143–47.

Colom, F., and D. Lam. 2005. Psychoeducation: Improving outcomes in bipolar disorder. *European Psychiatry* 20 (5–6):359–64.

Colom, F., E. Vieta, M. J. Tacchi, J. Sánchez-Moreno, and J. Scott. 2005. Identifying and improving non-adherence in bipolar disorders. *Bipolar Disorders* 7 (Suppl. 5):24–31.

DBSA (Depression and Bipolar Support Alliance). 2005. "Food and Mood" brochure. www.dbsalliance.org/site/PageServer?pagename =about_publications. Accessed on March 4, 2008.

Ewing, J. A. 1984. Detecting alcoholism: The CAGE questionnaire. *Journal of the American Medical Association* 252 (14):1905–7.

Fagiolini, A., D. J. Kupfer, J. Scott, H. A. Swartz, D. Cook, D. M. Novick, and E. Frank. 2006. Hyothyroidism in patients with bipolar I disorder treated primarily with lithium. *Epidemiologia e Psichiatria Sociale* 15 (2):123–27.

Frances, A., J. P. Docherty, and D. A. Kahn. 1996. Expert consensus treatment guidelines for bipolar disorder: A guide for patients and families. *Journal of Clinical Psychiatry* 57 (Suppl. 12A). Reprint, National Depressive and Manic Depressive Association (NDMDA), 1996.

Frank, E., J. M. Gonzalez, and A. Fagiolini. 2006. The importance of routine for preventing recurrence in bipolar disorder. *American Journal of Psychiatry* 163:981–85.

Frye, M. A., and I. M. Salloum. 2006. Bipolar disorder and comorbid alcholism: Prevalence rate and treatment considerations. *Bipolar Disorder* 8:677–85.

Garno, J., J. Goldberg, P. Ramirez, and Barry A. Ritzler. 2005. Impact of childhood abuse on the clinical course of bipolar disorder. *British Journal of Psychiatry* 186:121–25.

Goldstein, B. I., V. P. Velyvis, and S. V. Parikh. 2006. The association between moderate alcohol use and illness severity in bipolar disorder: A preliminary report. *Journal of Clinical Psychiatry* 67 (1):102–6.

Gonzalez-Pinto, C. Gonzalez, S. Enjuto, B. Fernandez de Corres, P. Lopez, J. Palomo, M. Gutierrez, F. Mosquera, and J. L. Perez de Heredia. 2004. Psychoeducation and cognitive-behavioral therapy in bipolar disorder: An update. *Acta Psychiatrica Scandinaviaca* 109:83–90.

Goodwin, R. D., and A. Marusic. 2006. Low sleep as a predictor of suicide ideation and attempt: A general population study. *Psychiatria Danubina* 18 (Suppl. 1):133.

Gutierrez, M. J., and J. Scott. 2004. Psychological treatment for bipolar disorders: A review of randomised controlled trials. *European Archives of Psychiatry and Clinical Neuroscience* 254 (2):92–98.

Gyulai, L., M. Bauer, M. S. Bauer, F. García-España, A. Cnaan, and P. C. Whybrow. 2003. Thyroid hypofunction in patients with rapid-cycling bipolar disorder after lithium challenge. *Biological Psychiatry* 53:899–905.

Jamison, K. R. 2000. Suicide and bipolar disorder. *Journal of Clinical Psychiatry* 61 (Suppl. 9):47–51.

Jones, S. H. 2001. Circadian rhythms, multilevel models of emotion, and bipolar disorder: An initial step towards integration? *Clinical Psychology Review* 21 (8):1193–1209.

———. 2004. Psychotherapy of bipolar disorder: A review. *Journal of Affective Disorders* 80 (2–3):101–14.

Kaplan, B. J., S. G. Crawford, C. J. Field, and J. S. A. Simpson. 2007. Vitamins, minerals, and mood. *Psychological Bulletin* 133 (5):747–60.

Keck, P. E., and S. L. McElroy. 2003. Bipolar disorder, obesity, and pharmacotherapy-associated weight gain. *Journal of Clinical Psychiatry* 64 (12):1426–35.

Kessing, L. V., E. Agerbo, and P. B. Mortensen. 2004. Major stressful life events and other risk factors for first admission with mania. *Bipolar Disorders* 6 (2):122–29.

Kessler, R. C., W. T. Chiu, O. Demler, and E. E. Walters. 2005. Prevalence, severity, and comorbidity of 12-month *DSM-IV* disorders in the National Comorbidity Survey Replication NCS-R. *Archives of General Psychiatry* 62:617–27.

Kilbourne, A. M., D. L. Rofey, J. F. McCarthy, E. P. Post, D. Welsh, and F. C. Blow. 2007. Nutrition and exercise behavior among patients with bipolar disorder. *Bipolar Disorders* 9 (5):443–52.

Kleindienst, N., R. R. Engel, and W. Greil. 2005. Psychosocial and demographic factors associated with response to prophylactic lithium: A systematic review for bipolar disorders. *Psychological Medicine* 35:1685–94.

Leitzmann, M. F., Y. Park, A. Blair, R. Ballard-Barbash, T. Mouw, A. R. Hollenbeck, and A. Schatzkin. 2007. Physical activity recommendations and decreased risk of mortality. *Archives of Internal Medicine* 167 (22):2453–60.

Leverich, G. S., and R. M. Post. 2006. Course of bipolar illness after history of childhood trauma. *Lancet* 367:1040–42.

Lin, P. Y., and K. P. Su. 2007. A meta-analytic review of double-blind, placebo-controlled trials of antidepressant efficacy of omega-3 fatty acids. *Journal of Clinical Psychiatry* 68 (7): 1056–61.

McDevitt, J., and J. Wilbur. 2006. Exercise and people with serious, persistent mental illness: A group walking program may be an effective way to lower the risk of comorbidities. *American Journal of Nursing* 106 (4):50–54.

McIntyre, R. S., J. Z. Konarski, K. Wilkins, J. K. Soczynska, and S. H. Kennedy. 2006. Obesity in bipolar disorder and major depressive disorder: Results from a National Community Health Survey on mental health and well-being. *Canadian Journal of Psychiatry* 51:274–80.

Miklowitz, D. J., and M. J. Goldstein. 1990. Behavioral family treatment for patients with bipolar affective disorder. *Behavior Modification* 14 (4):457–89.

Miklowitz, D. J., and M. W. Otto. 2006. New psychosocial interventions for bipolar disorder: A review of literature and introduction of the systematic treatment enhancement program. *Journal of Cognitive Psychotherapy* 20:215–30.

Miklowitz, D. J., M. W. Otto, E. Frank, N. A. Reilly-Harrington, S. R. Wisniewski, J. N. Kogan, A. A. Nierenberg, J. R. Calabrese, L. B. Marangell, L. Gyulai, M. Araga, J. M. Gonzalez, E. R. Shirley, M. E. Thase, and G. S. Sachs. 2007. Psychosocial treatments for bipolar depression: A 1-year randomized trial from the Systematic Treatment Enhancement Program. *Archives of General Psychiatry* 64 (4):419–27. In National Institute of Mental Health (NIMH). 2007. Results from the NIMH-funded systematic treatment enhancement program for bipolar disorder (STEP-BD). Accessed at www.nimh.nih.gov/health/trials/practical/step-bd/index.shtml on June 15, 2008.

Milano, W., F. Grillo, A. Del Mastro, M. De Rosa, B. Sanseverino, C. Petrella, and A. Capasso. 2007. Appropriate intervention strategies for weight gain induced by olanzapine: A randomized controlled study. *Advances in Therapy* 24 (1):123–34.

NIMH (National Institute of Mental Health). 2001. Bipolar disorder. Accessed at www.nimh.gov/publicat/bipolar.cfm on September 20, 2006.

Nierenberg, A. A., T. Burt, J. Matthews, and A. P. Weiss. 1999. Mania associated with St. John's wort. *Biological Psychiatry* 46 (12):1707–8.

Parker, G., N. A. Gibson, H. Brotchie, G. Heruc, A. M. Rees, and D. Hadzi-Pavlovic. 2006. Omega-3 fatty acids and mood disorders. *American Journal of Psychiatry* 163:969–78.

Paykel, E. S. 2003. Life events and affective disorders. *Acta Psychiatrica Scandinavica* 108 (Suppl. 418):61–66.

Peden, A. R., M. K. Rayens, L. A. Hall, and E. Grant. 2005. Testing an intervention to reduce negative thinking, depressive symptoms, and chronic stressors in low-income single mothers. *Journal of Nursing Scholarship* 37 (3):268–74.

Perlman, C. A., S. L. Johnson, and T. A. Mellman. 2006. The prospective impact of sleep duration on depression and mania. *Bipolar Disorders* 8 (3):271–74.

Preston, J., J. H. O'Neal, and M. Talaga. 2009. *Consumer's Guide to Psychiatric Drugs.* New York: Simon and Schuster.

Poulin, M. J., L. Cortese, R. Williams, N. Wine, and R. S. McIntyre. 2005. Atypical antipsychotics in psychiatric practice: Practical implications for clinical monitoring. *Canadian Journal of Psychiatry* 50 (9):555–62.

Rea, M. M., M. C. Tompson, D. J. Miklowitz, M. J. Goldstein, S. Hwang, and J. Mintz. 2003. Family-focused treatment versus individual treatment for bipolar disorder: Results of a randomized clinical trial. *Journal of Consulting and Clinical Psychology* 71 (3):482–92.

Reilly-Harrington, N. A., T. Deckersbach, R. Knauz, Y. Wu, T. Tran, P. Eidelman, H. G. Lund, G. Sachs, and A. A. Nierenberg. 2007. Cognitive behavioral therapy for rapid-cycling bipolar disorder: A pilot study. *Journal of Psychiatric Practice* 135:291–97.

Schneck, C. D. 2006. Treatment of rapid-cycling bipolar disorder. *Journal of Clinical Psychiatry* 67 (Suppl. 11):22–27.

Scott, J. 2003. Group psychoeducation reduces recurrence and hospital admission in people with bipolar disorder. *Evidence-Based Mental Health* 6:115.

Scott, J. 2006. Psychotherapy for bipolar disorders: Efficacy and effectiveness. *Journal of Psychopharmacology* 20 (Suppl. 2):46–50.

Scott, J., and M. J. Gutierrez. 2004. The current status of psychological treatments in bipolar disorders: A systematic review of relapse prevention. *Bipolar Disorders* 6 (6):498–503.

Slentz, C. A., J. A. Houmard, and W. E. Kraus. 2007. Modest exercise prevents the progressive disease associated with physical inactivity. *Exercise and Sport Science Reviews* 35 (1):18–23.

Smith, M. T., M. I. Huang, and R. Manber. 2005. Cognitive behavior therapy for chronic insomnia occurring within the context of medical and psychiatric disorders. *Clinical Psychology Review* 25 (5):559–92.

Srinivasan, V., M. Smits, W. Spence, A. D. Lowe, L. Kayumov, S. R. Pandi-Perumal, B. Parry, and D. P. Cardinali. 2006. Melatonin in mood disorders. *World Journal of Biological Psychiatry* 7 (3):138–51.

Strakowski, S. M., M. P. DelBello, D. E. Fleck, C. M. Adler, R. M. Anthenelli, P. E. Keck, Jr., L. M. Arnold, and J. Amicone. 2007. Effects of co-occurring cannabis use disorders on the course of bipolar disorder after a first hospitalization for mania. *Archives of General Psychiatry* 64:57–64.

Umlauf, M. G., and M. Shattell. 2005. The ecology of bipolar disorder: The importance of sleep. *Issues in Mental Health Nursing* 26 (7):699–720.

U.S. Department of Health and Human Services. 1999. *Physical Activity and Health: A Report of the Surgeon General.* Atlanta: U.S. Department of Health and Human Services. Accessed at www.cdc.gov/nccdphp/sgr/sgr.htm on January 8, 2008.

Wildes, J. E., M. D. Marcus, and A. Fagiolini. 2006. Obesity in patients with bipolar disorder: A biopsychosocial-behavioral model. *Journal of Clinical Psychiatry* 67 (6):904–15.

Williams, D. J., and W. B. Strean. 2006. Physical activity promotion in social work. *Social Work* 51 (2):180–84.